THE A. S. W. ROSENBACH FELLOWSHIP

IN BIBLIOGRAPHY

Bibliography and *pseudo*-Bibliography

by A. Edward Newton

PUBLICATIONS OF

The Rosenbach Fellowship in Bibliography

———

To A.E.N. with my love (April 1927)

Dear Caliph — I suddenly realize,
seeing this pamphlet again; why it
is that the author has no copy of
his own primary indiscretion. He
has no copy because he gave it to
you. But unless there were
testimony to that effect it might
be supposed that you had obtained
the pamphlet by sinister means.
And so dear Caliph I rededicate
to you this copy of a sheaf of
peccadilloes which, when
they were innocently committed,
never dreamed of reaching a
haven (or heaven) of editions and
bindings such as Oak Knoll. Your
very affectionate Kit Morley

Inscription in Morley's *The Eighth Sin*.

BIBLIOGRAPHY

AND

pseudo-

BIBLIOGRAPHY

———

by A. Edward Newton

Rosenbach Fellow in Bibliography

———

PHILADELPHIA:

UNIVERSITY OF PENNSYLVANIA PRESS

1936

Contents

I. Bibliography and *pseudo*-Bibliography

I AM *honored in being asked to give this course of lectures, but you will, I hope, not expect too much of me; remember that I am not a scholar, merely a collector—to quote Eugene Field, "I am one of those who seek what bibliomaniacs love." It is this passion which has led me to use as a frontispiece to this volume a reproduction of an inscription in a rare little pamphlet of exquisitely clever verse,* The Eighth Sin, *by Christopher Morley; his "primary indiscretion," he calls it; the same beloved Kit who had the honor, several years ago, of giving the first, and the best, of these lectures on bibliographical subjects on the foundation established by Dr. A. S. W. Rosenbach, the great bookseller—may the tribe increase.*

IN its simplest form bibliography concerns itself with the how and when and why and where and whence of books. Bibliographies are indeed not intended for average readers, be they gentle or simple. They are intended as tools for the scholar, weapons for the bookseller, and armor for the collector. Bibliography is, to me, an interesting subject, and I shall try to make it interesting to you; if I fail, as perhaps I shall, it will not be the fault of my subject; if you do not agree with my opinions you are not obliged to accept them; this is a free country—at least we have been told so often that it is, that we have come to believe it. My subject is not new; we have, however, in recent years approached it from a new angle: we interest ourselves in phases which did not exist for our ancestors. So many complexities have crept into it that some have ventured to call it a science—it may be so; values enter into it. Dr. Johnson, a saint in my calendar, has said, very truly, that the most valuable editions are the first; the most useful, commonly, are the last. Dr. Johnson's sayings have been divided into several classes: he talked to enlighten and inform; occasionally he talked for victory and frequently he talked for fun: for whatever reason he talked, no one ever talked better.

If, in the course of the three addresses which I am privileged to make, you find me wandering from the subject, as now, you will I hope forgive me, and Dr. Rosenbach especially will, I trust, accord me a little inattention, for I shall not keep strictly to the terms he has laid down. Rules were made to be broken, there are exceptions to all rules: I am an exception.

Bibliography concerns itself with things so minute that it sometimes leaves the broad highway of literature and wanders into bypaths in which it loses itself. When it is completely lost I call it pseudo-bibliography: let me explain: It is impossible to be too meticulous in the study of a great book, the Bible, say, or a First Folio of Shakespeare. When, however, a man begins to talk, as one did to me a few months ago in London, about a run of five or seven variants of the first editions of *The Prisoner of Zenda*, by the late Sir Anthony Hope Hawkins, calling, or seeking to call my attention to differences in punctuation or lettering on the title-page, to variations in end papers and to broken or

mutilated lettering on the cloth cover, it was with difficulty
that I could refrain from exclaiming, with Lear, "That way
madness lies: let me shun that." We should be reasonably
sure that a book or an author or a subject is worth intensive
study before we lose ourselves in it. "Dost thou love life?
Then do not squander time, for that is the stuff life is made
of," said Benjamin Franklin.

Questions of format aside, for the moment, the all-im-
portant thing in a book is what the author said or intended
to say. And if in the course of printing—or of publishing,
which is a different matter—he altered his text, it is perfectly legitimate for us to inquire how and to what extent
he changed his mind and to speculate as to what caused him
to do so. Now to get right down to dots; a book may derive
its importance from its subject or from its author. No one, I
suppose, would rank Mason L. Weems with James Boswell
as a biographer, but Weems was the first man to write a
Life of George Washington, and more than eighty editions
of his book have been printed; we cannot therefore ignore
Parson Weems. Boswell was important himself and Johnson was very important. Weems is important because he
was the first to write the life of a great man; I shall deal
with him at some length in my next address.

Further as to James Boswell. In the "Oak Knoll" Library
there is an unique copy of the first edition of his *Life of
Johnson* in two large quarto volumes. In every known copy
of Volume II, except the one referred to, page 302 is not
part of a signature, or quire as our English friends call it,
but the original leaf has been removed leaving a tiny stub
on which another leaf, separately printed, has been pasted;
unless one's attention is called to it this fact might pass un-

noticed. The matter canceled or deleted was a rather free discussion between Boswell and Johnson upon marital infidelity, a subject especially interesting to the biographer, who was notoriously a loose liver. Johnson, Boswell says, was in a very good humor on one occasion and in a moment of inadvertence told Boswell of Mrs. Johnson's amazing opinion of the subject, not expecting that her opinion would go rattling down the ages, as it certainly would have done had not Malone, without whose help and persistence the great book would hardly have been completed, insisted that the page be canceled and Johnson's remarks very considerably abbreviated and toned down. We should not be human if we did not wish to discover what was said that occasioned such a hubbub. A few of us knew because we had seen the offending passage in the proof sheets, which are the property of my friend Mr. R. B. Adam of Buffalo, but it was believed that not one single copy of the book, printed and bound, in which the offending passage appeared, was in existence; but to the amazement of all, such a copy turned up: the newspapers rang with the discovery, and the book came to America. Now, mark you, this is an important bibliographical discovery; the canceled, that is to say, the removed page—which the learned Dr. R. W. Chapman, Secretary to the Delegates of the Oxford Press, has decided shall be called a *cancellandum*—disappeared and a new page was printed and pasted on a stub in every copy of the book and bound, except the unique copy referred to; this inserted page Dr. Chapman calls a *cancellans*. Now turn we to Professor Tinker's Oxford Edition of Johnson's Letters (page 422), where Boswell wonders, with Malone, ". . . how you and I admitted this to the public eye? . . . It is, however, mighty good stuff"—these last words sound like Newton but they are not mine; I am still quoting James Boswell. This is bibliography; opposed to this is something quite unimportant found in the same book. A few years ago, someone in reading his Boswell in first edition came across the word "give" in which the letter "i" was lacking; the booksellers seized upon this "point," as it is called, and presently their catalogues began to suggest rather than to say that copies with the defective word "gve," of which there were many, were a first printing of the first edition. Recourse again was had to Mr. Adam's proof sheets, in which the word was fully spelled "give"; the inference being that in the course of printing the "i" had dropped out of the word, there was no means of telling to a certainty when or how. It was, in brief, a mare's-nest, of almost negligible interest: this is an example of pseudo-bibliography.

Midway between these two examples; between fresh air and folly, as it were, is this: Some years ago, in 1920 to be exact, Mrs. Edith Wharton, one of our best novelists—certainly the best in portraying New York society in what might be called the brownstone-front period—published *The Age of Innocence*. It had been serialized in a magazine which had an enormous circulation and was no doubt read by thousands, without comment. It was not until it was published in book form by Messrs. Appleton that an amusing blunder was discovered. It had escaped the author, several proof readers, and Mrs. Wharton's sister-in-law, Mrs. Cadwalader Jones, a very learned lady; that in a fashionable New York church banked with flowers, with bridesmaids in pink and ushers in black, with several rectors and a bishop in attendance, the officiating clergyman began the wedding

service by: "Forasmuch as it hath pleased Almighty God"
—which I hope all of you will recognize as the opening
lines of the paragraph of the burial service of the Episcopal
Church which includes "earth to earth, ashes to ashes, dust
to dust." The book had been out for some time when, one
day, an indignant clergyman wrote Mrs. Wharton to inquire if she did not know the difference between a wedding
and a funeral service! Slips of this kind are of frequent oc-
currence; they arise not from ignorance so much as from
knowledge. Mrs. Cadwalader Jones (from whom I have the
story), who will be known to old Philadelphians as the
daughter of William Henry Rawle, had been brought up in
all the sanctity of old St. Peter's and was no doubt letter
perfect in her Prayer Book. There is another slip in the
same book, in which Mrs. Wharton makes a famous violin-
ist, who has never been in this country, play at a fashionable
musicale in New York. Sarasate's name had to be substituted for Joachim's; it was a longer name—more trouble!—
an overrun of one letter.

Every great book when first published literally teems
with errors, perhaps the First Folio of Shakespeare more
than any other, although the address, "To the great Variety of Readers," if it were modernized in spelling, might be
mistaken for the blurb of a book-of-the-month club, so up
to the minute are Messrs. Heminge and Condell, with their
fantastic statement that "what he (Shakespeare) thought,
he uttered with that easinesse, that wee have scarce received from him a blot in his papers." Having in mind the
fact that Shakespeare took, or seems to have taken, little or
no interest in the printing of his plays, and that the First
Folio was not published until 1623, when he had been lying

in the chancel of Stratford Church for seven years, this statement admits of no defense, and Ben Jonson was quite right when he expressed the wish that his friend had blotted a thousand. The birthmarks of the First Folio were removed to some extent in the Second Folio, but Sidney Lee says that when an old misprint was removed a new one was introduced, so that blunders are almost as numerous in the Second Folio as in the First.

In the brief three or four hours I may hope to detain you with this lecture I shall not have time to display my ignorance of the Elizabethans; of the good or bad Quartos, so called, of Shakespeare, or of the poets or dramatists of the Restoration—for two reasons: first, because I know nothing about them (one should go to Henrietta Bartlett for such information), and second, they are hardly as yet being subjected to the scalpel of the modern bibliographer, who has begun, one might say, with books of the present time and worked backwards. But I cannot refrain from speaking of a "point" in a folio which has just been discovered by Professor Robert M. Smith of Lehigh University. In a recent number of *The Colophon*, he has a most interesting article. Few scholars can write amusingly on bibliographical subjects: Professor Smith is one of the few; his story, briefly, is this. Many years ago, in England, an unique proof of a title-page of a First Folio of Shakespeare came upon the market. It was unique in several ways: there were peculiarities about the famous Droeshout portrait, and, more important, after the word "copies" in the line "Published according to the true original copies," there was a colon, whereas on all other title-pages this word is followed, as it should be, by a period. Bibliographers and scholars went mad—frequently they have not far to go; presently this item came to America. Marsden J. Perry got it, then Dr. Rosenbach acquired it, and finally, of course, Mr. Folger; now it belongs to the Nation. While Mr. Folger was assembling in New York his amazing Shakespearean collection he was too busy selling Standard Oil to all and sundry to bother about showing his treasures to inquisitive scholars. He was one of the busiest of men; year after year he devoted the day to business, the night to the purchase of Shakespeare; scholars must wait his pleasure, their turn would come. But somehow or other a photograph or a photostat was made of the title-page, and in either a dark reddish-brown dot comes out as black as jet, and it was not until the magnificent Folger Shakespeare Library was thrown open to the public and scholars were permitted to examine its treasures that Professor Smith, examining the colon under a magnifying glass, discovered the upper dot of the colon to be a forgery—made by a little fly; in other words, a flyspeck, of which there are clearly several on the title-page. "Then I, and you, and all of us fell down." It may be that some villain, worse than a murderer, has done us dirt and that the dot was made by a pen, but Professor Smith says it was not one of Jaggard's colons, and no one doubts him. Pope's couplet comes to mind:

> Why has not man a microscopic eye?
> For this plain reason, man is not a fly.

Here is a case of a fly doing the work of a man.

But we are not yet done with colons. Last year in the American Art Association Anderson Galleries there was a rare Shelley item sold, of which the catalogue says: "The present copy displays a colon after the word *Epipsychidion* on the title-page. There seems to be no doubt that the colon was an oversight on the part of the printer and was deleted in the second issue published the same year."

And yet again, and finally: I have myself flirted with a colon. In the very learned *Bibliography of Robinson Crusoe*, of my friend Henry Clinton Hutchins, to which I contributed an introduction, I observed the immense care with which Hutchins had tracked certain words, like "apply" and "pilot" and their variations, from place to place; then, no doubt to allow himself a little relaxation, he pointed out the technical difference between editions and issues, which is a most intricate matter. Presently I observed that a part of the plot seemed to turn on a colon; this tempted me to say,

How amazed Defoe would be if he could take up this Bibliography and follow the fortunes, not of Crusoe and his man Friday, but a mere word through several pages and finally how a matter of life and death seems to hang upon a mark of punctuation, a colon—not that unpleasant thing we carry about in our insides—or even half a colon.

I am afraid that Professor Hutchins thought this *infra dig.* in a serious study which had occupied him for ten years. But he graciously permitted my harmless little joke.

It is the habit of printers to make hash of one's copy, right down to the present day. A friend of mine, Paul Lemperly, a bibliographer by the grace of God, wrote to Professor A. E. Housman, seeing that a new edition of his famous book, *A Shropshire Lad*, was announced, saying: "I highly value my copy of the first edition; is there anything new important in your last?" To which the weary and slightly irritable scholar replied, "No, only a few new blunders replacing the old ones." This *Shropshire Lad* is one of the most highly prized books of modern verse—I don't quite know why, for I like my poetry drawn mild and not too much of it. Last summer in England I picked up a tiny reprint for eighteen pence and carried it in my vest pocket on a motor journey and read the book carefully. The verses are neat rather than gaudy; pat, exact, faultless in rhyme and meter, certainly the best words in their best order, but they are not especially beautiful nor do they compel thought, except the first poem, "1887," the year of Queen Victoria's Jubilee when everyone was singing and saying "God Save the Queen." Here is Housman's last verse:

> Oh, God will save her, fear you not:
> Be you the men you've been,
> Get you the sons your fathers got,
> And God will save the Queen.

This is excellent: when a thought is finely stated one can say more in four lines of poetry than in ten lines of prose— and they are remembered more easily.

Dr. Rosenbach will certainly regard this as a digression, but my appointment cannot be withdrawn, and in these lectures I shall reserve the right to leap from point to point, from peak to peak as it were, and this brings me back to Dr. Johnson, a very high peak indeed. In his most characteristic poem, *The Vanity of Human Wishes*, published several years before the Dictionary, occur the famous lines:

> There mark what ills the scholar's life assail,
> Toil, envy, want, the *garret* and the gaol.

But when his Dictionary had been published, Johnson, smarting under the neglect of the great Earl of Chesterfield, changed the last line so that it should read:

Toil, envy, want, the *patron* and the gaol.

Johnson always wrote *currente calamo*, with a flowing pen, but second thoughts are sometimes best. As first printed there was a sentence in his *Journey to the Western Islands of Scotland* in which his indignation at the desecration of a cathedral by the removal of the lead which covered its roof, that it might be converted into money for the pay of the army, led him to rejoice that the vessel that carried this cargo was lost at sea, in which rejoicing he hoped his readers would join him. The thought of this desecration carried him even further; it appears that at some time it had been suggested that the lead on the roof of the cathedral in his native city of Lichfield be used for some profane purpose. In his indignation the Doctor wrote: "What they shall melt it were just that they should swallow." The reproduction of the page on which this violent statement appears may be seen in Courtney's *Bibliography of Johnson*, but it became a cancel. My copy being bound, the cancellandum does not seem to be upon a stub, but it is, nevertheless, and it may be observed that the paper is several shades darker than the leaves immediately preceding and following it.

May I refer to Johnson's *Rasselas*, as it is commonly called?—written in the evenings of one week to defray his mother's funeral expenses. It will be remembered that this story was called by its author *The Prince of Abissinia* spelt with an "i." Abyssinia, spelt with a "y," is very much in the public eye at the moment; it is a part of ancient Ethiopia; its population is mongrel and the people have inherited from the Copts of Egypt a form of Christianity in which worship of the Trinity is, I am told, an important part. Very well, Dr. Johnson knew all this and much more, for his first book (not his first literary work) was a translation from the French of *A Voyage to Abyssinia*, by Father Lobo, a Portuguese Jesuit. For this substantial piece of anonymous work Johnson received the munificent sum of five guineas. And when he wanted a locale for his "gloomy fable," as it has been called, he placed his Prince in a happy valley in which he could want for nothing: that presently became his complaint—he wanted to want something. In a recent issue of *The Saturday Review*, for which our friend Kit Morley writes so delightfully, he makes a shrewd guess "that the name Rasselas should probably be written as two words, Ras Selas"; Ras, he says, is probably an Ethiopian prefix of honor. Ras Selas evidently means something not unlike Prince Selassie. It does. Ras, an eminent scholar in this city tells me, means Prince, and moreover, Prince of the Trinity. And I venture the belief that very few of the Abyssinians who see those monstrous Italian aeroplanes hovering over them, filled with "northern savages" dropping bombs and poison gas upon them—poor wretches—know that Dr. Johnson makes an Abyssinian, eminent for his knowledge of mechanic power, deliver himself of a homily on aeroplanes in these words:

If men were all virtuous I should with great alacrity teach them all to fly. But what would be the security of the good, if the bad could at pleasure invade them from the sky? Against an army sailing through the clouds, neither walls, nor mountains, nor seas, could afford any security. A flight of northern savages

[13]

might hover in the wind, and light at once with irresistible vio-
lence upon the capital of a fruitful region that was rolling under
them. Even this valley, the retreat of princes, the abode of hap-
piness, might be violated.

And this, be it remembered, was written by a meditative
philosopher in an attic, in London, one hundred and seventy-
seven years ago.

When authors write at white heat, they frequently occasion their censors, official and otherwise, and subsequently
their bibliographers, a good deal of difficulty. In reading an
article on Heinrich Heine recently—that fiery particle of
which Germany stands in need today, as never before—I
came upon this blistering reference to Napoleon. After re-
ferring to him as an upstart Corsican—the phrase has passed
into history—Heine made reference to his marriage with
Marie Louise, the proud and beautiful daughter of the Em-
peror of Austria, in these words (I quote from memory):
"That Revolution Incarnate, which booted and spurred and
spattered with the blood of battle, mounted the bed of an
imperial blonde and polluted the pale sheets of the House
of Hapsburg." This sonorous period, if it lacks something
of the dignity of Gibbon, has nevertheless the rolling, oce-
anic quality which sticks it in one's memory like a phrase
from Macaulay—that is, it would have done so if the censor
had not deleted it. As printed it lost more than half its sting.

Not far from where Dr. Johnson lived in Gough Square
was The Temple in which Oliver Goldsmith lived, he who,
in the phrase of the famous epitaph, "touched nothing that
he did not adorn." To have written the best poem, the best
play, and the best novel of his generation, with honorable
mention in other fields, is indeed marvelous. Let us first

consider *The Deserted Village*. On the 26th of May, 1770, the *Public Advertiser* printed the announcement: "This day, at twelve, will be published, price two shillings, *The Deserted Village*, a Poem by Dr. Goldsmith"; twelve days later a second edition appeared, and the week following a third. "This man is a poet!" exclaimed the author of *An Elegy Wrote in a Country Church Yard*. All this would seem to be clear enough, but what of three tiny little "privately printed" editions, at least one of which Temple Scott, the bibliographer, says was issued in December 1769, although dated on the title-page 1770? One of these little books, 24 pages, 7 by 4⅛, is before me as I write. (Mr. William M. Elkins of this city has all three.) How do we know which is the first? Well, the first line on page 9, "Amidst thy bowers the tyrant's *head* is seen," becomes "Amidst thy bowers the tyrant's *hand* is seen" in all subsequent issues, including the quarto or the twelve o'clock edition—there you are, as right as rain. It is interesting to remember that Boswell tells us that Dr. Johnson wrote the last four lines of this poem.

Turn we now to *She Stoops to Conquer: or, The Mistakes of a Night*, published in 1773. Bibliographers are not yet in accord as to just what and how many blunders are requisite for a first issue of a first edition; they are as plentiful as blackberries. As the book went through the press, corrections were made, and for one blunder corrected two were introduced. One may think, if one chooses, that the typesetters were indeed celebrating "the mistakes of a night." In the "Oak Knoll" Library there is a slender, unbound pamphlet of fifty pages, 6½ by 4 inches, which I believe may antedate all the accepted Newbery editions, and may be valuable or quite worthless. Its title-page says it was "Taken from The Manager's Book at the Theatre Royal Covent Garden." It was printed in London for R. Butters, No. 79, Fleet Street; no date is given and it has no dedication, prologue, or epilogue, nor are the dramatis personae for the most part those with which the play is associated.

Well known is Dr. Johnson's abuse of Oliver Goldsmith —but he would permit no one else to abuse him. "Is there a man now living who can pen an essay with such ease and elegance as he?" And after his death: "Let not his faults be remembered, he was a very great man." The simplicity and modesty and beauty of the Dedication of *She Stoops to Conquer* to Dr. Johnson is not always remembered: "By inscribing this slight performance to you, I do not mean so much to compliment you as myself. It may do me some honour to inform the public, that I have lived many years in intimacy with you, etc."

One more Goldsmith item and we shall move on more rapidly: *The Vicar of Wakefield.* The story of its writing, of its author being arrested for debt, his rescue by Johnson, and the sale of the manuscript; all this is well known, but why the delay of almost four years in its publication, and why was it printed in Salisbury and not in London? An echo answers, Why? There are said to be four variants of the first edition; which mine is, I do not know and I do not much care. You see, really, Dr. Rosenbach should have hired an honest-to-God bibliographer to give these lectures rather than a man who gets more pleasure out of reading the book than finding blunders in it; for blunders a book must have— to interest a bibliographer. In *The Vicar*, catchwords must be incorrect or omitted altogether, and Wakefield must be

spelt variously "Waekefield" or "Wakfeild" or "Wak-
fild." In the second edition some of these mistakes are corrected, but Goldy by this time had lost interest; speaking
of it to a friend, he said, "Newbery gave me sixty pounds
for the copyright and had I made it ever so perfect or correct I should not have had a shilling more." Sixty pounds—
three hundred dollars! for the manuscript of *The Vicar of
Wakefield*, with the right of publication. What would it be
worth today? When Jerome Kern's copy of the first edition
sold in 1929—that time when Wall Street had transferred
itself to the auction room—a copy of the book, said to be a
presentation copy (but this was questioned), brought six
thousand six hundred dollars! I love presentation copies
but I do not find myself possessed of an inordinate desire to
get a book in so fine a state as to make its price practically
prohibitive. I ask only for a good, sound copy of a desired
item in the condition, as nearly as may be, in which it was
published. I do not want it in binding, however fine; but
when I am asked to pay perhaps twice as much for a volume
with its spine and paper label intact—supposing that was
its original condition—as I am for the same volume showing some signs of wear, I content myself very comfortably
with the less fine item and spend the money thus saved on
something else. After all, it is important to remember that
books are one thing, bric-a-brac is another. We collectors
are not sufficiently catholic in our tastes; "high spots"
(damn the phrase) are, too often, evidences of limited men-
tality. In support of my position I call in evidence Carroll
A. Wilson of New York: let him be cross-examined.

In the introduction to Geoffrey Keynes' charming little
Bibliography of Jane Austen he speaks with sense and sen-

sibility of the emotion engendered in the heart of book-binders a century ago when they saw a half-title, which he calls—and with reason—"the crowning grace of a book." "They almost always ripped them out," he says, "and copy after copy comes down to us lacking the half-title." Indeed so insistent are we on half-titles that obliging or wicked booksellers sometimes insert them in books that never had them; "Americans like them," they say. *It is always well to leave a book in whatever condition it comes to one—no matter what that condition may be. I have seldom bound a book but that I regret having done so.* People are always asking questions which cannot be answered when a book has been re-bound; e.g.,—Is the title-page or a half-title part of a signature? Is there a cancel on a stub of some given page? How was the book bound originally? If the book you have acquired is a rare one, such as a *Paradise Lost*, with a first title-page, put it, if you wish, in a fine solander case, or a cloth "fleece-lined box," or, if necessary, wrap it up in a piece of brown paper and tie it with a string; in short, do anything with it except bind it. Any experienced collector or bookseller will indorse this judgment.

There are all sorts of bibliographies; making a bibliography is, in the words of Geoffrey Keynes, a method by which one can express one's homage to the genius of an author; for the doing of the job is its own reward. Dr. Johnson calls a dictionary-maker a harmless drudge. I wonder what he would call Michael Sadleir or Mrs. Luther Livingston. Their respective Bibliographies of Anthony Trollope and Rudyard Kipling are marvels of learning and monuments of patience. My own choice is for a bibliography which one can read with pleasure, such an one as Pottle's

Literary Career of James Boswell, Esq. rather than the stark scholarship of Mrs. Livingston.

Some of you will remember the little nonsense couplet which we used to recite to one another forty years ago, looking forward to that time

> When the Rudyards cease from Kipling,
> And the Haggards ride no more.

Well, I fancy Mrs. Livingston, as she sat down with the data out of which she made this amazing bibliography before her, wished that Rudyard had ceased his Kipling and found his place in the Abbey earlier. I know nothing about them but I have a feeling that Mrs. Livingston's work must teem with errors; sins of omission and sins of commission —how could it be otherwise? Here is a big volume, five hundred pages of fine print, for the most part; attempting to track down five hundred items, newspapers, pamphlets, magazines, and books printed during the last fifty years in all parts of the world—for no writer of our time compares in popularity with Kipling. This very popularity makes him difficult; there are pirated editions and trick editions to secure copyright, and things like them innumerable.

In the "Oak Knoll" Library there are half a dozen rare Kipling items; I shall not refer to them, but ask you to join me in singing "The Absent-Minded Beggar": page 225 of the Bibliography. This poem first appeared in *The Daily Mail*, October 31st, 1899; then appeared a little pamphlet issued probably for recruiting purposes. On November 13th, to the music of Sir Arthur Sullivan, it was first sung at the Alhambra Theatre in London, by Mr. John Coates. I knew him slightly; my wife played his accompaniments once at a ship's concert. On November 25th, seventy-five thousand copies, five leaves fastened with blue ribbon, words and music were printed; entire proceeds to soldiers and sailors of all arms and grades in actual service. Do I tire you? We have not started yet; on and on it goes; pages of it. George Eliot said that she began to write *Romola* a young woman and when she had completed it she was an old one; yet I should say that her novel was a pleasant holi- day task compared to Mrs. Livingston's Bibliography—for bear in mind that she received from Kipling the same meas- ure of help for her work that the editors of the First Folio received from Shakespeare. My friend Ellis Ames Ballard of this city, who has one of the finest Kipling collections in the world, has been engaged for some years in the prepara- tion of an account of it; a copy reached me on Christmas Day. I shall talk to you about it in my next lecture which will be entitled "Book Catalogues." Mr. Ballard knows his Kipling as Macaulay knew his Archbishops of Canterbury, forwards or backwards; and there is his friend, and mine, Admiral Lloyd H. Chandler of Washington with his *Kipling Summary* and the rest, who could, and does put Kipling's knowledge of himself to very shame. Kipling was not too easy to get along with; he was a good hater. He hated many things and most men, especially Americans: he thought we were a dull, money-loving race, easily fooled, motivated by slogans. We would try to lionize him and he grew tired of being lionized; he would not meet people and he would not have his portrait painted, not even by Augustus John, for the National Portrait Gallery. He was the last of the giants; when he died he left England with no outstanding literary figure, unless it be Bernard Shaw, the playboy who has the serious purpose of amusing us. To return to "The Beggar." My wife and I happened to be in London in the autumn of 1899 when it was all the rage; there never had been anything like it. It was sung at every performance, in every theatre in town for months. Hansoms—there were no taxis then—could not pass rapidly through the streets for the crowds singing it; every barrel organ played it, and long after midnight a tenor or a bass or a soprano could be heard chanting:

> Will you kindly drop a shilling in my little tambourine
> For a gentleman in khaki ordered South?

And we did, constantly—everyone did. It is said that a hundred and fifty thousand pounds were raised; such is the power of song. The Boer War got off to a good press in England; people were as convinced of the justice of their attack on the Dutch of South Africa as today they are convinced that the Italians, who are only doing what the English did a generation ago, are wickedly and shamefully attacking the Abyssinians; and the English did not have the same excuse.

But it is time for me to return to bibliography. A very pretty discovery was made right here in our own library not long ago by William M. Sale, Jr. of Yale University. He discovered in the Godfrey F. Singer Collection of Eighteenth Century Novels an unique copy of Samuel Richardson's *Sir Charles Grandison*. In every copy examined, including the "Oak Knoll" copy, page 350 of Volume II is on a stub; the cancellandum is, however, found in the Singer copy, which makes it unique. Through an error the corresponding leaf in Volume III was canceled. Through the courtesy of our librarian, Mr. Thompson, I have been able to place several interesting photostats in my copy of *Sir Charles*, and I am quite sure that other collectors of famous English novels will be glad to do likewise. I have never read *Sir Charles Grandison*. *Pamela* delights me; one can make fun of it—I have. I have also read *Clarissa Harlowe*, it is inexpressibly tedious but a tragedy hardly less poignant than *Romeo and Juliet*. I am not sufficiently robust to take on *Sir Charles*, although, may I whisper it? I have a presentation copy in boards uncut.

I wish that I were competent to speak of Scott, the great Sir Walter, bibliographically. He is the idol of my friend William C. Van Antwerp, whose collection of the works of "the man who was a man, if God ever made one"—in the words of Stanley Baldwin—is the finest in existence. Scott's books are a puzzle; in a recent issue of *The Colophon*, a quarterly magazine which must appeal to every booklover, David A. Randall quotes from a speech of John Hay when he was unveiling a bust of Sir Walter in Westminster Abbey, as follows:

I have heard from my father-in-law, a pioneer of Kentucky, that in the early days of this century (that is now the last century) men would ride from all the neighboring counties to the principal post-town when a new novel by the author of *Waverley* was expected.

The books they awaited so avidly were pirated editions published by several houses in New York and Mathew Carey of this city, of whom we shall hear something in another connection. They sought by fair means and foul, chiefly foul, to get advance sheets of forthcoming novels from Edinburgh, and from these set up their rival reprint, striving to get ahead of one another in their enterprise. Carey, we are told, when his edition was ready to market, chartered a stagecoach and galloped day and night to awaiting booksellers in New York. But the novels produced in such haste—by employing every printer available, the job could be done in three or four days—were by no means identical with the novels given to British readers. Scott wrote under great pressure; to preserve his anonymity his manuscript was not sent to the printer but was copied by an amanuensis, and galley or page proofs subjected to careful revision; these changes did not appear in the first American editions; hence their interest for students today. Greville Worthington, in London, another friend, now forsaken the book trade to become a stock broker, and no doubt a good one—if any such there be—devoted the leisure of several years to the discovery of what was a true first edition of any given novel by Scott, in the course of which innumerable cancels came to the surface. And just here let me say that to a scholar like Dr. R. W. Chapman of the Oxford Press, there is no such thing as a "trifling" discovery; "it is not for the bibliographer to decide what is important, his business is to record the facts," he says. This being the case, a rebound copy of a book is put out of court by that very fact—cancels are difficult or impossible to discover; is the half-title a conjugate leaf? (there is a new word) and only by tearing the book to pieces, which a collector is loath to do, can these and like questions be answered.

Waverley is, of course, the rarest of Scott's novels—an honest confession is said to be good for the soul: I have never read it nor do I own a copy of the first Edinburgh

edition. Worthington, who devotes some eighteen pages
to the study of it, says it appeared on July 7th, 1814, and
only one thousand copies were printed; no wonder it is
exceedingly scarce, as is also my copy of the New York
edition, printed and published by Van Winkle and Wiley,
Corner of Wall and New Streets, in 1815. My copy has a
manuscript note which reads: "This is the identical copy sold
to an English collector by Lathrop C. Harper of New York
some years ago. Mr. Harper has never seen another copy."
I bought it from William H. Robinson, 16 Pall Mall, in
1930. It is in two volumes (not three, as is the Edinburgh
edition), boards, uncut, labels gone, and alas! the spine is
broken. Some day someone will wish to examine it; Mr.
Randall most likely: he's welcome to. After *Waverley* came
Guy Mannering, of which two thousand copies were printed,
followed by *The Antiquary*, with six; after that, the deluge.
One of the reasons that the English Novel is now attracting
the attention of collectors and bibliographers alike is its human interest. People buy poetry to put away or to give
away; poets don't buy poetry to read, they read their own
—and usually prefer it. As Coleridge wrote to Wordsworth, "The great majority of buyers of new volumes of
poems read at least twenty novels for one of poetry." If
that was true a hundred years ago it is still more true today;
good novels on their appearance were read to shreds. Last
autumn a copy of *The Last of the Mohicans* fetched at auction in New York thirty-one hundred dollars! The novel, as
I pointed out a few years ago, is a comparatively new and
certainly a fertile field for collector and bibliographer alike;
let us come to Thomas Hardy.

He first published an article that appeared in *Chambers's*

Journal for March 18, 1865, entitled "How I Built Myself a House," but magazine articles are only now beginning to count largely in bibliography, and his first novel, as everyone knows, was *Desperate Remedies*. Now just here I want to make a point as to which some will disagree with me. It is the habit of some to stress unduly the color of the cloth in which an important novel is bound. One man says a book must be bound in red, another in green, another in blue; dependent, too frequently, upon how his copy is bound, if he has one to sell, or upon the copy he owns, if it be upon his shelves. Is the cloth pebbled or smooth? And what about the end papers? another will inquire. These matters are of interest but not always vital; chasing such points leads one into many mare's-nests. My *Desperate Remedies* is bound in red; all that I have seen are similarly bound, except one. A year ago, I spent a day very pleasantly with Mrs. Thomas Hardy at Max Gate, Dorchester; by chance asked her to show me her copy of this famous book, famous because it was Hardy's first novel and is scarce. Out it came, a presentation copy to the first Mrs. Hardy and bound in grass green cloth. Someone tells me that a certain book should have a heavy black line with rounded corners on the side, and the cloth rough; another authority demands the corners square and the cloth smooth. How can points such as these be told to a certainty? Publishers and binders do not keep accurate records of these matters, which at the time of publication seem unimportant.

> The play's the thing,
> Wherein I'll catch the conscience of the king.

For "play" read "text," and if we would pluck out the heart

of the mystery of the book, let us confine ourselves chiefly to the text of the author and we shall have enough to do. Mistakes, some of them amusing, some of them fatal to sense, are to be found in almost every first edition. In the first edition of Charles Reade's *The Cloister and the Hearth*, Volume II, page 372, there is a sentence which reads: "Catherine threw her face over her apron and sobbed," and is there not a *not* omitted from one of the Commandments in a certain edition of the Bible, which got the printer into a lot of trouble? The word *road* for *load*, Volume III, page 198, is one of the distinguishing marks of a first edition of *Tess of the D'Urbervilles*, in which there are also several words with transposed letters, but canceled pages and pages substituted therefor are the items of real interest.

As time rolls on Thackeray yields his place, or does it only seem to me so? Be this as it may, Charles Dickens remains, in my judgment, the supreme English genius since Shakespeare. By reason of the publication of most of his important books in parts—the accepted manner of his day—they afford a fertile field for the bibliographer. I shall refer only to *Pickwick*, in the study of which I have had a hand. Several years ago, my friend John C. Eckel of this city asked me to write an introduction to his bibliography which I suggested be called

Prime Pickwicks
in Parts

Census
With Complete Collation
Comparison and Comment

which, I submit, is a very pretty bit of alliteration. *Pickwick* celebrates its centenary this year, in March; it is one of the great books of the world. Mrs. Livingston in her *opus* is severely self-denying; not one word of comment or illumination comes from her. Mr. Eckel is not so austere. "The standing," he says, "of *The Posthumous Papers of the Pickwick Club*, to give the book its full and complete title, has never been successfully challenged. Its birth was coincident with the beginning of the reign of Victoria and the literature produced during the lifetime of the great Queen has been surpassed, if at all, only by that era that we call Elizabethan. And at the very pinnacle of all the works of the Age of Victoria stands Charles Dickens' remarkable book, *Pickwick Papers*, written by a young and almost unknown journalist; certainly the ways of genius are inscrutable." Thus the keynote is struck, but there are many instruments in the orchestra; wrappers, text, illustrations, all must approach a standard, and remember the form of its publication, monthly parts for nineteen months, the last part being a double number; remember too that only five hundred copies were printed of the first two parts, and perhaps only three hundred of the third, at which time the book almost expired; and that, thanks to the young genius getting his stride and the happy conjunction of Samuel Pickwick with Sam Weller, ten, fifteen, perhaps thirty thousand copies of the last parts were printed, and we can understand why a "prime" *Pickwick* in parts is a valuable possession. "A fine *Pickwick* is like a fine yacht in a close race, until the time allowance is carefully figured no one knows who wins. . . . It is a magnificent thing to qualify for the race at all." I felt very much set up when Mr. Eckel announced my qualifications.

The papers that have been written and read on *Pickwick!*

One of the latest is from the pen of the distinguished "Bencher of the Inner Temple," Sir Frank Mackinnon, of whom it may be said, "What he don't know isn't knowledge." Having reread Jane Austen with the keenest understanding, assisted by a map, a road book, a calendar and a thermometer, and finding the glorious Jane never makes the slightest blunder in any of her details, he turns to *Pickwick* and finds nothing else. "Dickens," he says, "dashed off his manuscript with a fine disregard of—everything, and produced a masterpiece." His characters, conversing in July 1827, speak of occurrences which actually took place in 1830! Mr. Pickwick talks of doing something "next day," which is actually a Sunday, and then goes on to describe something which could only happen on a week day. He describes a walk on a pleasant afternoon in June, whereas if one follows carefully the account of each day since the Club began its peregrinations it is certainly still May. But what difference does it make if the chronology of *Pickwick* is wrong from start to finish? and he ends his very learned and witty article this way:

Let no one suppose that, when I note inaccuracies or anachronisms, I do so by way of depreciation; or that, if I compare the studied accuracy of Jane Austen, it is a comparison of merit rather than of method. No one ever derived more delight from *Pickwick* than I. If the old hypothesis—the nightmare of a single book upon a desert island—were to be propounded, and the choice limited to either *Pickwick* or *Pride and Prejudice*, I think I should have to toss up!

There is catholicity for you! Janeites are not always Dickensians and at the same time Justices of the King's Bench.

The English delight in pictures that tell a story and love

a verse that says something—so do I—these of Kipling for instance:

Jane lies in Winchester—blessed be her shade!
Praise the Lord for making her, and her for all she made!
And while the stones of Winchester or Milsom Street remain,
Glory, love and honor unto England's Jane.

I quote from memory—any fool can quote with a book before him.

With *Pickwick* I shall introduce a phase of bibliography which is of the utmost importance and which, perhaps, should have been touched upon before; namely, the fashion and format of the book. In the early days of the printed book, if the book was a substantial one, the sheets were assembled and sewn into leather covers over oak or elm boards; otherwise sheets of paper were pasted together which later became pasteboard, and covered with leather. The question of placing the title of the book did not at first arise; when it did, it was lettered in ink on what we now call the spine, then the spine became ornamented by gilt tooling, which included a title; finally, to make it more prominent, the title was placed upon a leather label of a contrasting color. I have elsewhere called this the age of CALF. We are moving rapidly through several hundred years; books became common and cheap, and in the effort to produce a book at a low price, the leather covers gave way to pasteboard covers merely with titles printed on white paper labels pasted on the spine. In flimsy pasteboard covers were bound the novels of Jane Austen and Sir Walter; I have called this the age of BOARDS. But a few years before the time when the Pickwick Club set out upon its peregrinations a new fashion obtained. Novels and some other books were published without any binding whatever; they were, in fact, pamphlets, published monthly, frequently with illustrations printed from copper plates; sometimes these illustrations were colored by hand: an especially fine example of this period is the *Comic History of England* and the *Comic History of Rome* with their exquisitely humorous pictures by John Leech. It is well known that the text of *Pickwick* followed distantly the first illustrations by Seymour, but the genius of Dickens soon asserted itself and the illustrations became subordinate to the text. With the age of PARTS the bibliographer's work settled down into an all-time job. The "points" which have to be considered in acquiring or perfecting a first edition of *Pickwick* which would pass the scrutiny of an expert have become sufficiently bewildering in number and extent, without including slips of paper of various colors on which are printed advertisements of such things as Beulah Saline Water and Rowland's Macassar Oil. These are not integral parts of the book. No one can say with any certainty that every copy of any given part contained all the slips which mad bibliographers say are required for perfection. Authorities differ; but by what means does one become an authority? Certainly not by merely having a copy for sale. If this course is persisted in, nine-tenths of all books in parts may become valueless; this would be a great pity, for many get great enjoyment out of collecting them. Rowland's Macassar Oil was the proprietary name of a very popular hair-oil, and we get the blessed word "antimacassar" for a covering, later called a "tidy," which was thrown over chairs, sofas, etc., to protect them from the grease. *To say that no copy of a book in*

parts, or any other book, is "right" unless the advertisements are
in order, is folly; unless, be it well understood, the advertise-
ments are an integral part of the book.

Finally, after a brief but happy reign, PARTS gave way
to the three-volume novel, the THREE DECKER it was
called. Books in general, and novels particularly, well
printed on good paper, with woodcut illustrations by excellent artists, well and frequently handsomely bound in
cloth, became the style. The circulating libraries dominated
this era: they indicated the fashion and they set the price;
the three volumes cost one and a half guineas, and so rigid
were the libraries in their demands that when Emily
Brontë produced *Wuthering Heights* in 1847, although it
filled only two volumes, it was announced as in three on
the title-page, the last volume containing another novel by
another sister, Anne, and the novel, *Agnes Grey,* an in-
nocuous little tale of no merit whatever. We all feel today
that we understand *Wuthering Heights,* and perhaps we do,
but Charlotte Brontë did not, and in the second edition
which she prepared for the press she mitigated, somewhat,
its asperities. It is, indeed, only since the new edition of
the Oxford World's Classics Series has been printed that
we have the book as it appeared originally in the first
edition.

When Robert Ross, the friend of Oscar Wilde, was
asked to write an introduction to the two-volume *Bibli-*
ography of Wilde, compiled by a man who called himself
Stuart Mason but whose proper name was Christopher S.
Millard, he said among other things that in turning the
proofs for ten minutes he had learned more about Wilde's
writings than Wilde himself ever knew; and then went on

to quiet the apprehension of anyone who might approach these two big volumes, casually, by saying that they are not nearly as dull as they look. Nor are they; they were, indeed, hailed upon their appearance, now more than twenty years ago, as a new form of bibliography. Ten years were devoted to the compiling of it; it was ana and bibliography rolled into one, most comprehensively. I shall not speak of it in further detail for the reason that the "Oak Knoll" Library is not sufficiently strong in Wilde material to enable me easily to do so; moreover, Stuart Mason merely set a fashion that other bibliographers like Frederick A. Pottle and Michael Sadleir have followed since. To return to Ross's statement that Oscar Wilde knew little of his own bibliography: this, I think, is true of all authors. There is a saying that those who can, do, and those who cannot, teach. A great productive writer is too busy with his creative work to chase a comma, a colon, a date, or an elusive quotation over a ten-acre lot, and it is too frequently, of such infinitesimal things as these that bibliography consists. If I may be pardoned I shall refer to a personal experience. On the 11th of November 1918—I remember it was Armistice Day—I published my first book, *The Amenities of Book-Collecting;* several of the essays therein had previously been published in *The Atlantic Monthly,* and it was not until the book had been set up that someone wrote the Editor telling him that I had made a slip in placing the Carlton Hotel, in London, in Piccadilly rather than, where it is, in Pall Mall. Did I want a cancel leaf? I well remember my disgust. "No," I said, "print a little errata slip with these words thereon and insert it opposite the offending page.

Page 268: The author has made a slip of the pen in locating the Carlton Hotel in Piccadilly and not on the corner of Pall Mall and the Haymarket. His attention has been called to it, but he preferred to leave the blunder as it was—and is—as a sort of lightning rod for critics, to divert their attention from—possibly —probably—more serious blunders.

It never entered my mind that *The Amenities* would enter a second edition, much less a fifth or sixth, or whatever it is, and that this harmless little errata slip would become a "point," sought as one of the birthmarks of the first edition. I have told the story as I remember it for the reason that George H. Sargent makes no mention of it in the *Newton Bibliography*. This handsome and quite unnecessary book was almost privately printed (only one hundred and ten copies), by a group of friends, Dr. Rosenbach, George H. Sargent, Kit Morley and others, who kept their nefarious counsel so well that I knew nothing of it until on Christmas Eve, 1927, Rosy summoned me to his office, as in great haste, and handed me the volume. I was, of course, much touched—as what amateur author would not be? and I shall only refer to one line of it, the first, in which the compiler uttered at least one great truth: "There is a certain absurdity in starting upon such an undertaking" (as this).

I should not have introduced American literature by reference to such an unimportant item, but I find it difficult to become enthusiastic over much of our national literary production; we are a great manufacturing nation—a reading rather than a writing one. Indeed our really important authors may be counted on the fingers of one hand. First is Poe, whose place seems secure. From a bibliographical point of view, his *Tamerlane*, quite worthless as poetry, is the rarest American item in literature—if ten foolish and fugitive poems may be called literature. His *Tales* are highly esteemed wherever good English is read, and his poetry is sonorous and beautiful, whatever it may mean. His *Poems*, second edition, New York, 1831, is really the first; he merely called it a second edition to make people believe that it was selling. My copy was once his.

Hawthorne, who may be a much greater novelist than we now think him, is represented by one book, *The Scarlet Letter*. His *Fanshaw* is negligible from a literary point of view. Its author tried to suppress it and it is excessively rare, but *The Scarlet Letter* which depicts, critically, the life of Puritan New England, is a very fine novel. The catchword of the first edition, *reduplicate*, line 20, on page 21, becomes *repudiate* in subsequent editions. Emerson, a deity fifty years ago, now becoming outmoded as a philosopher, may possibly come back, for philosophy is a circle and not a straight line. Walt Whitman is represented by *Leaves of Grass*. Not everyone knows that Walt was the author of a novel, *Franklin Evans, or the Inebriate*, "by a popular American author," the title-page tells us. Popular, forsooth! I am afraid that Walt began by being a fraud and kept it up. It antedates *Leaves of Grass* by thirteen years and is very rare. Whitman is the poet of Democracy, in which one's confidence has been rudely shaken these last few years. There remain Melville, the author of *Moby Dick*, and Samuel Langhorne Clemens, best known the world over as Mark Twain. I ask your attention to *Moby Dick*.

This great book was written by a curious and enigmatic man, Herman Melville, when he was thirty-one years of age. He had written several excellent books before *Moby*

Dick, but he wrote nothing of importance afterwards. When he had turned over the manuscript to Harper Brothers in New York his creative work was done, yet he lived forty years longer; his royalties were negligible, and for twenty years he was a clerk in the Custom House; dying in 1891. *Moby Dick* is the best sea story ever written; it is also a colossal allegory worthy of the pen of Bunyan or of Swift. Hawthorne, to whom it was dedicated, did not understand it; indeed few of us do as yet. But it is as a bibliographical item and not as a work of art (an English critic has called it the finest thing written in English since *Paradise Lost*) that I wish to discuss it. It appeared under the title by which we know it in New York, in 1851, in one volume. It was published in London by the Bentleys the same year, as *The Whale*, in three volumes. The London edition antedates the New York edition by a few weeks and is excessively rare. A copy was bought a few weeks ago by Sessler in this city for fifteen hundred and seventy-five dollars, and immediately sold, no doubt at a substantial profit. Dr. Rosenbach, many years ago, paid ten dollars for the dedication copy: he has it in his own private library, from which nothing has ever emerged. In *The Atlantic Monthly* for October 1931, in speaking of this book I said that I had been told that the three-volume London edition is shorter than the one-volume New York edition and it would be interesting to compare the two texts. I let it go at that; where I ended I should have begun. A few months later I received a letter from Professor William S. Ament of Scripps College telling me that he and his wife had compared the texts of the two editions and found enough material to make a magazine article and, let me add, a most interesting one from which I quote, with generous omissions: The book was written, as so many great books are, by a poor man on the verge of a nervous breakdown. Apparently each section of the manuscript was sent to Harper & Brothers, by whom it was given to the printers, who, in turn, shipped a set of proof sheets to Richard Bentley in London, who gave it to some blockhead for such editing as would make it desirable for English readers; he did not hesitate to rewrite whole sentences, to omit what he considered crude or blasphemous passages, and in particular he omitted one whole chapter, a short one to be sure, in which Ishmael speculates on the coronation stuff with which a king's head is solemnly oiled. What can it be? he asks. Certainly not olive oil, nor bear's oil, nor train oil, nor cod liver oil (not even macassar oil); what can it possibly be but whale oil, and sperm at that? Where is the divinity that doth hedge a king if questions such as these be asked? And saddest of all, perhaps, we learn from the London edition that "Alas! all fish have very vague ideas of the connubial tie": this in lieu of the statement in the New York edition that "an old bull whale cannot keep a young Lothario whale out of his bed, for alas! all fish bed in common." It's enough to make one shun even a salted mackerel, forevermore. If one is known by the company one keeps, do we not become part and parcel of what we eat?

So our greatest book was "Bowdlerized" to make it fit reading for a Victorian maiden aunt, and words which occur in novels today without let or hindrance are represented by dashes or are emasculated beyond recognition; it was the custom of the time. I was much struck by this when reading, quite recently, a very great novel of the late Victorian era, *Robbery Under Arms,* by Rolf Boldrewood (a nom de plume:

his proper name was Thomas A. Browne). It is a tale of the Australian bush country, and was published in 1888, in London. It is indeed Australia's one magnificent contribution to literature. Most of the men are thieves and murderers, and the ladies of easy virtue, I feel sure, yet there is not in all three volumes a word, in what purports to record their conversation, which could not be repeated in the presence of Queen Victoria herself.

Anyone who stops to think of the difference between the Victorians and ourselves will be perplexed at the squeamishness of our ancestors. I am not prepared to believe that there is less chastity today than there was when the Queen came to the throne, or shortly thereafter, but certainly our manners and customs and costumes are very different. Women formerly had "chests" and had no hesitation in showing them, but they were presumed to be entirely without legs and seemingly ran about on castors. Even as lately as twenty-five years ago, women playing tennis at Wimbledon did so in long skirts which swept the ground or would have done so had not the skirt been slightly raised and carried in the left hand. Today modesty in young women has practically disappeared. "Show me a modest woman and I'll show you an ugly one," remarked a handsome young Amazon, who reclining in a steamer chair was smoking vigorously, in a single garment which I believe is technically known and well described as a "short." No longer will a young woman balk, as did Miss O'Grady (in *Handy Andy*) at being shut up in a room with a man without any clothes, and seek refuge under the bed. "Beds are made to get into, not under," she would doubtless say. But I must not pursue the subject further.

In 1850, Thackeray writing the preface to *Pendennis*
says: "Since the author of *Tom Jones* was buried, no writer
of fiction among us has been permitted to depict to his utmost power a MAN. We must drape him, and give him a
certain conventional simper," and he goes on to say that he
has been penalized for even suggesting that young men are
subjected to certain temptations when they go out into the
world. Trollope's bold, bad men are the most mealy-
mouthed of mortals; there is not a good manly DAMN or
a robust GO TO HELL among the whole lot of 'em. But in
nothing as much as in the use of tobacco have times
changed. "I like to see a man enjoy his cigar in the open air
after dinner," remarks the Victorian young lady, anxious to
show how prepared she is to make concessions to masculine
weaknesses, and I have in mind the story of the statesman
who was found sitting on the floor of his bedroom at Wind-
sor Castle blowing the smoke of his cigar up the chimney,
in mortal fear of discovery by his Sovereign. Today the lady
will light her cigarette as soon as the law allows, and as she
makes the law, she lights it promptly.

One final word on *Moby Dick;* I leave the subject reluctantly. A friend of mine, William S. Gleim, of Rohrerstown,
Pennsylvania, a most learned Melvillian, has written a
treatise on the allegorical or symbolic meaning of the book
which, in my judgment, is our greatest contribution to
literature. His *Theory of Moby Dick* is too profound for me
but I respect it: I always respect what I do not understand:
it is a good rule.

I have mentioned Walt Whitman as one of the great
figures in American literature: this is what I am told rather
than what I believe. Democracy and the brotherhood of

man are themes for the politician or the poet, and in the judgment of neither do I set much confidence, but *Leaves of Grass* is interesting bibliographically. The poet is said to have set a part of the type of the first edition himself, and the long lines of his verse look rather well on the wide page of the edition, published in Brooklyn, in 1855. Carolyn Wells, whom years ago I set collecting Whitman when she wanted to get in the book-collecting game, says in the Check List which she made with the assistance of Alfred F. Goldsmith, that it is unlikely that all the *Leaves of Grass* printed were bound at once, as the second issue lacks the gilt edges and the gold lines on the covers of the first. The second issue, too, has some pages of favorable press comments of the first issue bound in; these notices are said to have been written by Whitman himself. It is quite likely, for no movie star, lamenting the loss of a million-dollar necklace, was a better self-advertiser than the poet. The "Good Gray Poet" kept himself much in the public eye; he was a noble-looking old man, very clean, and he "handled," as he called it, his *Leaves* himself and was not above accepting alms from friends and admirers. I used frequently to see him walking, meditatively, the streets of Philadelphia, and I bought at least two copies of *Leaves of Grass* from him, personally, in Camden. When he died I was one of several thousand who attended his funeral. It was supposed that he was very poor at the time, but not so; he had hived enough of this world's wealth to buy for himself a handsome and costly tomb in Harleigh Cemetery—now a place of pilgrimage.

To return to the *Leaves*. The second edition, Brooklyn, 1856, has a quotation stamped in gold letters on the spine of a dumpy volume: "I greet you at the beginning of a great career. R. W. Emerson." This was taken from a private letter written by Emerson and was one of the few unsolicited tributes the poet received. But Emerson was not well pleased thus to appear as sponsor for the *Leaves*, at that time considered so shocking that even the publishers, Fowler and Wells, declined to put their name on the title-page. When, some time later, Whitman got a job in the Department of the Interior at Washington, he was promptly fired by the Secretary when it was discovered that he was the author of *Leaves of Grass*, and as late as 1881 the District Attorney of the City of Boston threatened booksellers with criminal prosecution unless the poem was expurgated. It is said that Whitman sent Whittier a first edition, which the author of *Snow-Bound* instantly put in the fire. Wendell Phillips' comment was, "All sorts of leaves except fig leaves."

Speaking of fig leaves reminds me of a run-in I had several years ago with our own Treasury Department, which accused me of seeking to import "lewd and filthy material." I, of course, indignantly denied the charge and was told that the offending importation was a copy of Rabelais. In the course of the correspondence I addressed the following letter to Uncle Andy Mellon:

The action of your representative is positively glorious! Rabelais is one of the world's classics: it is no more obscene than are Shakespeare and the English Bible. In order that you may not be the laughingstock of the world, I beg that the volume be sent to me immediately; but for no other reason, for one can secure a copy at any well-ordered book-shop or library in the United States.

I am not a youth seeking to gloat, surreptitiously, over a smutty book, but a student of mature years, the possessor of an important library, and the author of *The Amenities of Book-Collecting*, *A Magnificent Farce*, *Doctor Johnson* (a play), *The Greatest Book in the World* (a study of the Bible), *This Book-Collecting Game*. Moreover, I have a copy of the first edition of Rabelais, which is worth several thousand dollars.

If you keep or destroy my Rabelais, it will be in my power to make you and your department ridiculous the world over. This would afford me much greater pleasure than the possession of the book.

The upshot of it all was that the book was taken from me and I was made to "pay sixty-nine cents postage to return the offending volumes to the country of their origin." The price was remitted. Meantime there was no reason why the book should not be printed and sold in this country; the crime was in the *importation*! But this is gossip—pseudo-bibliography with a vengeance.

When looking at a book, bibliographically, one feels like saying, as one frequently does when one meets a person of twenty whom one has not seen for ten years: "How you have grown!" When John Eckel published his Bibliography of Charles Dickens back in 1913, he said, speaking of the *Christmas Carol*, "It has just enough bibliographical twists to make it interesting." With the passage of years we find what once appeared simple has become very complex indeed. In like manner the two or three points which we once thought embraced the difficulties of Mark Twain's *Huckleberry Finn* have become many. We used to talk of blue cloth or green, of page 283 being on a stub and of a dropped figure 5 on page 155, and there ended the matter, but so no longer.

Merle Johnson, the inventor of the expressive but nauseating phrase, "high spots," says that there are fifty copies in green cloth to one in blue, and Irving S. Underhill, who has devoted years to the study of *Huck*, places the book on what he calls a "dizzy peak of bibliographical eminence"; from this bit of eloquence one may judge how he feels about it. He has told his tale at intervals, each time adding corroborative detail. From him we learn that thirty thousand copies of the first edition were printed, certainly enough to go round. Soon we are told that the bust of the author which appears on the leaf between the frontispiece and the title-page has become important, and that there is the defective word "been" in the last line on page 319, also the whole story of the mutilated illustration on page 283 which made it so "obnoxious" that the publisher, Charles L. Webster, offered a reward of five hundred dollars for the apprehension and conviction of the miscreant who with an awl or graver did the dirty job. That two hundred and fifty copies had been shipped to San Francisco before the indecency was discovered; that western binders took apart and inserted a new illustration in their two hundred and fifty copies; and finally, that we shall find, as I well believe, in a home of mental invalids the bibliographer who has attempted to solve these and other mysteries—that we shall know him by his wild and startled look. And how, I ask you, will he be affected when he is told, as he may be, that after all this fuss and fury, the London edition, 1884 on the title-page, a much smaller book bound in *red* cloth, antedates the New York edition, dated 1885, bound sometimes in half morocco, occasionally in sheep, more frequently in blue cloth, and very commonly in green? "Do dates on title-pages mean anything?" you ask. "Sometimes, not always," is the correct answer.

Mark Twain was a great man, a sincere man and, what is rarer, a great humorist. Of tragedy we have more than enough. *Huckleberry Finn* is one of the world's great books, and its author's spoken witticisms seem destined for a long life. "The reports of my death are grossly exaggerated." "The lowest form of animal life is a Congressman." "Every one is talking about the weather, no one is doing anything about it." It is only when he left his proper field that he approached failure. His art sense was negligible and his literary judgment frequently unlucky. "Any library is a good library which does not contain Jane Austen." He loathed Fenimore Cooper, and Dowden's *Life of Shelley* roused his ire, as well it might.

And now comes to my library table a most disconcerting volume entitled *Anglo American First Editions*, describing first editions of English authors whose books were published in America before their publication in England. Here's a how-d'ye-do, a pretty mess, a state of things indeed, if our English editions of Barrie, Carlyle, Collins, Dickens, Haggard, Hardy, Reade and others, have to give way to cheap and nasty publications, enlarged pamphlets rather than books, printed in bad type on worse paper, bound, if at all, in the flimsiest manner. I cannot think that a "Seaside Library" edition or a publication by Munro made to sell for ten or twenty cents, or a publication by J. & J. Harper, for a dollar, will ever take the place of the handsome book in three volumes well printed on good paper, perhaps illustrated and substantially bound. *I admit that a first edition is a first edition, wherever published.* I admit, too, the pleasure of the chase for these waifs and strays of literature is enhanced by its difficulty; but who, armed with experience, knowledge, and taste, after a long hunt in a foreign field, will care to bring home not a lion or stag of ten, but a dead mouse—one of these poor, wretched, ragged examples of a pirate period. What am I to do with my copy of *The Woman in White* in three fine volumes, or my *Far From the Madding Crowd*, in two? Discard them? Not likely. The English booksellers in the future, as in the past, will have it both ways. I cannot think that bootleg liquor will take the place of vintage wine.

I have reached the end of my paper and my audience has listened to me very patiently. I shall take my place on this rostrum a week from today, to talk on Book Catalogues, with less trepidation.

II. Book Catalogues

I HAVE chosen the subject of Catalogues—book catalogues, of course—for the reason that it permits me to range from one subject to another at my own sweet will; for nothing changes its subject so often as a book catalogue, unless it be a dictionary. You remember the story of the man receiving a dictionary as a present; after he had read in it a little while, he insisted upon lending it to a neighbor; the neighbor returned it promptly (something very seldom done with a borrowed book) and was asked if he enjoyed it.

"Very much," he replied, "but I should have liked it better if it had not changed the subject so often."

The room in which this is written is almost full of catalogues of one sort or another: all are interesting to the book lover. There are catalogues of libraries large and small, there are catalogues of books on special subjects, there are book auction catalogues of famous sales past and of sales to come, and there are booksellers' catalogues—not publishers catalogues, mark you, for these are of little interest compared with those slender pamphlets of so-called secondhand booksellers which reach my desk from all over the world, literally by hundreds. In addition to catalogues, people try to sell me books by letter—sometimes I get as many as half a dozen in a day—asking me to buy some perfectly worthless book or batch of old books, for the idea that a book is old at a hundred years, and that all old books are valuable, will not down. And among the letters, sometimes, there is one asking if I will tell the writer how he—or she—can get a copy of the British Museum Catalogue and what will it cost? Anyone who has looked into the British Museum Catalogue will remember that it would fill, uncomfortably, this auditorium.

And this brings me very nicely—I hope you'll think—to a little catalogue, an acorn from which has grown a mighty oak. I have before me a tiny, slender pamphlet which I believe to be excessively rare. It was printed in Washington City in April 1802, by William Duane, and its title-page reads: *Catalogue of Books, Maps and Charts belonging to the Library of the Two Houses of Congress.* It is, in other words, the first catalogue of what is now the Library of Congress; it will repay examination. It is divided, as English sale catalogues still are, into folios, quartos, octavos, and duodecimos; each book or set of books is given a number and "its value as near as can be estimated." Including the duodecimos and excluding the maps and charts, of which there are nine, there are something less than a thousand volumes, and their estimated value is four thousand and fifty-seven dollars! The catalogue is interesting from another angle: for the books which are listed and for its omissions; it is, nevertheless, a fairly well-selected list. There are a good many volumes of history, including Gibbon, Robertson, and Hume, and I never think of history without thinking of Gibbon's definition of it. "History is little more than the register of the crimes, follies and misfortunes of mankind." There are a fair number of dictionaries, but omitting Dr. Johnson's, of which at the time there was a copy of the first edition in the Library of this University presented to it by Benjamin Franklin. Boswell is represented by his Journal, which is the volume we now call his *Tour to the Hebrides*; it is the gayest volume in his famous *Life of Johnson*, which is omitted. Smith's *Wealth of Nations*, Jefferson's *Notes on Virginia*, have a place, as has also Blackstone's *Commentaries on the Laws of England*, four volumes, the estimated value of which is twelve dollars, a low price if it was a first edition; from three to five hundred dollars is its price today.

From this small beginning grew the great Library of Congress with its, today, just under five million volumes and pamphlets, not including maps, charts, and manuscripts of which there are millions more. It is one of the great libraries of the world; only the Secretary of the Treasury, who is accustomed to hurling astronomical figures at us, would attempt to estimate its value. Its librarian, Dr. Herbert Putnam, is an outstanding figure; he has made the institution what it is. Librarians do not grow on trees, and the reason is not far to seek. They must rival railroad presidents as executives, have sympathy with and a trace of scholarship in all its branches, speak several languages and read several more, be prepared to suffer fools, gladly, from dawn to midnight—after that their time is their own. All this for the wage of a good "bookkeeper" in the ordinary sense.

The British, who talked much of the barbarity and savagery of the Germans during the Great War, and of their destruction of the great Library at Louvain, do not care to be reminded that during the War of 1812 when they occupied Washington they set about destroying our Library as it then was. In brief, they set fire to it and but for the effort of two assistant librarians it would have been totally destroyed. These men were instructed to pack such books as they could and convey them to a place of safety. It was easier said than done, but they did with great effort secure the use of a cart and four oxen, and in it "books, papers and records were carried to a safe and secret place in the country nine miles away." According to tradition, the Library was entirely destroyed, but as we have seen, several loads of books were saved. "Saved," but what became of them? Nobody knows. Great indignation was expressed throughout the country at this burning of the Library; even the English newspapers condemned the act, among them the editor of a paper published at Nottingham, who said that it was "an act without example in modern wars or in any other wars since the inroads of the barbarians who burnt Rome and overthrew the Empire." For thus commenting, the editor was accused of libel; with what result I do not know.

After the departure of the British and the establishment of peace, Thomas Jefferson offered to sell to the nation his library upon such terms as the Congress might dictate. He had previously thought of giving his books to the University of Virginia, but the destruction of the Library of Congress suggested an opportunity for its replacement. Jefferson made a generous offer and Congress, then as ever running true to form, proceeded to debate. "Too much money," said one. "Too many books in foreign languages, especially French," said another. "I understand it contains the writings of Voltaire, Rousseau and Locke—no doubt highly speculative in character," said a third. Congressman King of Massachusetts thought that a committee of Congress should "select"—fancy a committee of Congress selecting a library! The great Daniel Webster, I regret to say, thought this an excellent idea. Finally the library was purchased, January 30th, 1815—6,487 volumes for $23,950.00. Then the newspapers talked of folly and extravagance! Today this library is one of the nation's most valued possessions: it is preserved in the Rare Book Room under the direction of Mr. Valta Parma. For these details I am indebted to Mr. Julian P. Boyd, the accomplished librarian of the Historical Society of Pennsylvania, an institution of which every Pennsylvanian should be proud.

May I refer briefly to another public library, this time a small one, and then we shall, perhaps, get down to our subject. In 1667 Samuel Pepys made the following entry in his now famous Diary: "Home, and to my chamber and there finished my catalogue of books." Pepys, besides running the English Navy and running after pretty women, was an ardent book collector. I am not sure that I have ever seen any of the Catalogues of Pepys' Library—he made several, with the assistance of his wife and Deb Willett, the pretty servant wench that Pepys was given to hugging and kissing until one day Mrs. Pepys caught them in the act and turned the poor girl out of the house; wives of book collectors are so unreasonable. With all his philandering Pepys was a most methodical man, constantly arranging and rearranging his books, as good collectors do; there is hardly a pleasanter occupation. At his death he left his library to his nephew, John Jackson, and I have an autograph letter to the said John requesting him if he buys any prints for his uncle "to get very good ones only, but no books for of these as you know I have good plenty." And so he had, three thousand volumes, and he left the most careful directions as to their care. After his nephew's death they were to go with the curious old mahogany presses, made especially to contain them, to Magdalene College, Cambridge, and if that college did not follow his instructions to the letter, the library was to be forfeited and become the property of the college across the street. Needless to say that no instructions for the care of books have ever been more scrupulously observed. The books are arranged upon their shelves in double rows, the small books in front, the tall books behind, in exactly the same order that the Diarist placed them two hundred and fifty years ago.

You will by now have observed that I can neither write nor speak impersonally; for this weakness I apologize once for all. When I was twenty, that is to say before most of you were born, I chanced to spend a fortnight's holiday in the Poconos. There by great good fortune I met a delightful old gentleman, Ferdinand J. Dreer, of this city, at that time and for long afterwards a mighty autograph collector and an extra-illustrator of such books as pleased him. He took a fancy to me and we spent many hours together; he taught me much. One day in reminiscent mood he told me of the sale of the library of a friend of his, John Allan, which took place in New York, after his death in 1864. Allan was a Scotchman, born in Ayrshire; he came to New York, made a little money—not much—bought and amused himself throughout a long life by extra-illustrating books—a practice of which I do not approve, but let that pass. Dreer became his disciple, and I, Dreer's; so by the laying on of hands, as it were, my bibliographical life goes back, shall I say a hundred and fifty years? After the sale of Allan's library, the Bradford Club—named after an early Philadel-

phia printer, who emigrated to New York where he became famous—the Club may have passed by now, I do not
know—published a Memorial of John Allan, recording his
amiable personal qualities and his achievements in his avo-
cation. I bought a copy of this one night many years ago at
an auction sale, and read with interest an account of the sale
of his library; how the proceedings were occasionally inter-
rupted by the noise of a passing regiment leaving New York
to join the Union Army, for the Civil War was on. The
outstanding incident of Allan's book-collecting life was his
purchase through a friend of a Kilmarnock Edition of
Burns' *Poems*. I should like to tell the story. Every Scotchman wishes to own a copy of Burns; Allan wanted the famous Kilmarnock Edition, and seeing one in an English
catalogue, priced eight guineas, he wrote for it; when his
letter arrived the book had been sold and Allan was greatly
disappointed. Some time later, a friend, returning to Scotland from New York, asked Allan if he could do anything
for him in the old country. "Yes," was the reply, "if ever
you can, buy for me a Kilmarnock Burns."

"For how much?"

"You may have to pay ten guineas."

Ten guineas for a book! A year later, his friend, who was
an engineer, observed one of his workmen very drunk; it
must have cost money to get so tight, how did he get the
money? The question was asked.

"Oh, I pawned a Burns' *Poems* for ten shillings."

"What edition?"

"An old Kilmarnock that had been knocking around the
house for years."

Here was the desired opportunity. Allan's friend tried to

[52]

buy the pawn ticket for ten shillings, the old drunk wanted twenty, finally took fifteen and at that price the Burns passed into Allan's hands in New York. When his library came to be sold all attention was riveted on the Kilmarnock Burns, for the story was well known. What would it fetch? You will wish to know, I hope. It brought the unheard-of price of one hundred and six dollars! Only a few weeks ago while I was revolving in my mind the subject of this address I picked up the catalogue of a New York bookseller, Philip C. Duschnes, and read this:

BOOK AUCTION CATALOGUE. Books, Autographs, etc. belonging to the late John Allan. An interesting Catalogue of the early days of American book-collecting. 5,278 lots. 343 pages. Priced.

I at once sent for it and on its arrival enjoyed some pleasant hours in noting the change in fashion in book collecting. Books which today would fetch nothing brought much, and books which today bring thousands went for a song. For example, at the sale of Jerome Kern's books in 1929, his Kilmarnock Burns brought nearer seven thousand dollars than six. But remember that the price of a book, be it high or low, never tells the whole story. What condition is the book in? Condition is everything, except perhaps style; for there are fashions in books as in everything else. A book may be as out of date as a bustle, or the black alpaca polonaise which gave our grandmother such a pleasant thrill when it came home from the dressmaker fifty years ago. Allan thought that his sale would net about twelve thousand dollars; the realized total was $37,689.26. Let us turn the pages of Allan's catalogue for a moment. An Eliot Bible brought eight hundred and twenty-five dollars. It should now bring from six to eight thousand. I need hardly tell you that an Eliot Bible—to give you its proper title I should have to speak in an Indian dialect—is printed in an Indian language, and I very much doubt if the proof reader was not its last, perhaps its only reader. It was printed in 1661 in Cambridge, Massachusetts, and was a favorite book of King Charles II, not to read but *to give away*. It is only interesting as a curiosity and as the first Bible printed in what is now the United States.

The first *book* printed is *The Bay Psalm Book*, as it has come to be called; it is the rarest and most valuable book printed on this side of the Atlantic; Dr. Rosenbach's copy is the finest known; the one in the Boston Public Library is in dreadful condition. What a gloomy lot the people of Massachusetts were two or three hundred years ago! Their favorite book of poetry was the Reverend Michael Wigglesworth's *Day of Doom*. My copy is the seventh edition, published in 1751; it tells in awful verse how with a crash of thunder and a flash of lightning Judgment Day came and pretty much everyone went quick to eternal torment; unbaptized women and children first, but "to them the easiest room in hell," because their crime is less. I could not in my most exalted moment exaggerate the horror of this best seller for almost a century. Pray pardon this long digression; like the chorus girl I was led—I did not go astray.

To return to John Allan's sale catalogue. The Eliot Bible was not the high price of the sale. Irving's *Knickerbocker's History of New York*, extra-illustrated by 275 plates, and most elegantly bound, brought twelve hundred and fifty dollars; perhaps today it would fetch one-quarter this sum. And a Pickering *Angler*, two volumes extended to four, brought six hundred dollars. And so on. Today, unless you want to see your books slaughtered at auction, do not extra-illustrate them; keep them as nearly as possible in the condition in which they came from the publisher; and if you want prints and autograph letters, as you well may, keep them in a portfolio. When my old friend Dreer died, he left his autographs to the Historical Society of Pennsylvania and his books were sold at auction. I bought a fine extra-illustrated *Memoirs of Nicholas Biddle*, containing twenty-eight autograph letters from Penn, Franklin, Jefferson, Marshall, Webster, and others, and innumerable inlaid portraits, and pencil sketches of houses long since disappeared, for two hundred and eighty dollars—much less than the price of the letters had they been sold separately. Randolph Adams, a bibliographer and historian of high repute, says: "The reading of book-sellers' catalogues is one of life's highest pleasures." He is quite right, but there is as much difference in catalogues as there is in cats. Many go into the waste-paper basket unopened; others go upstairs to bed with me. I wish I could name names but it would not be fair, besides, one man's meat is another man's poison. But I find reading catalogues in one's library excessively stimulating: one is constantly getting up, running about, searching for a book, or otherwise attempting to verify a "point" or a price. I prefer to read them in bed: one's only care is not to disturb one's wife; from four to half-past five in the morning is my favorite time. If it be the part of wisdom to let a sleeping dog lie, what shall be said of the man who so switches on his light as to arouse his lady? Some day an electric eye will be discovered which will light a lamp merely by passing one's hand through the void.

As this book goes to press, an admirable catalogue reaches me from an eccentric and learned bookseller, George Bates, who keeps a shop in Shepherd's Market, London. Shepherd's Market is a quaint and curious little slum just off Piccadilly, right in the heart of Mayfair. I, like Nicodemus, go to see George by night: I discovered him that way several years ago when prowling about in search of a public house called "The Running Footman." This is how George expands over the first book of the For- syte series, a series which I venture to predict will "come back" and come back to stay.

GALSWORTHY (John) THE MAN OF PROPERTY. *Heine- mann*, 1906.

FIRST EDITION, cr. 8vo., orig. cloth, very slight wrinkling of cloth on spine. A FINE COPY, bright, clean and sound £24/–/–

* Despite assertions to the contrary, I am positive that there are no issue points whatever with this title. All genuine first editions con- tain the broken bar on page 200; all have inset sub-titles, and all have the last leaf as a separate sheet numbered "24" at foot. All copies that do not agree with this collation have, I am certain, been tam- pered with. The book having appreciable value, and second editions being in similar format, it is obvious that the book could and would be faked by using a clean second and inserting a correct first title from a soiled first.

With the second edition the sheets were re-arranged, all three sub- titles forming a part of the sheet concerned. This, it will be seen, gave a straightforward collation in eights, with the last gathering (num- ber 24) in four, and the key number "24" does not, therefore, appear on the last leaf but on the fourth from the end.

If care is exercised, faked copies are easy to detect, for the different

*collation of a second or third will always cause the faker to stumble.
If, for instance, in addition to inserting title and preliminaries from a
first into a second the last leaf is also removed, and a first edition leaf
inset, thus giving it the required test at foot of "24," it will be trace-
able on turning back three more leaves, where another "24" will be
found. No matter how far back the faker may go, the nigger will remain in the woodpile. If, on the other hand, only a second edition
cover is used on a first edition book, traces of recasing will show, and in
any event, it should be remembered that whereas you can get a book
clean inside and dirty outside, that it is obviously impossible for a
book to be clean outside and dirty inside, except in the case of an oc-
casional stain.*

*The broken bar is intact in the second edition and those that follow
until the Forsyte Saga sixteen years later. In this the bar is again
broken, the reason being that in preparing the book it was printed from
photographic blocks taken from the file copy of the first edition.*

Another modern "first" which has received the attention
of the faker is Conan Doyle's *Adventures of Sherlock Holmes*,
now become, in good condition, a scarce book. Here the
cloth cover is important; there are no points of issue with
this book, so far as I know. The difference between the first
and the second edition is when the signboard on the design
of the Strand on the front cover was given an inscription
reading "Southampton Street": the first edition covers have
this board left blank. Not infrequently soiled sheets of the
first printing, which have been further sophisticated by a
title-page on a stub, are bound in fresh covers of the second
edition. There are many similar pitfalls designed to entrap
the unwary. With all the care you may exercise, when your
library comes to be sold, if such should be its fate—it is not
an unhappy one—it will probably be discovered that some

bookseller has put one over on you. One! Many a one. How many Certain Nineteenth Century Pamphlets has not our market been called upon to digest? *Certain Nineteenth Century Forgeries* should be the title of Messrs. Carter and Pollard's excellent book which describes in such detail as would have delighted Sherlock Holmes the most remarkable series of fakes ever printed. The London booksellers who sold them to us at fantastic prices seem to think that their possession should be borne in dignified silence. I am not of this opinion. If I owned many of them (I have only an unimportant one, *Brother and Sister*), I should scream to heaven—or to hell, which is, no doubt, the permanent address of the forger or group of forgers. We know now whence they came but I note with indignation that an English trade journal is trying to suggest that these forgeries, of which a Reading (England, 1847) *Sonnets from the Portuguese* has several times sold for over a thousand dollars, emanated from America—the wish is father to the thought.

A few weeks ago in a catalogue I saw an item that I had long wanted, Weems's *Life of Washington*. I talked to Dr. Rosenbach about it. He said "I'll give you a copy." It had, I think, belonged to his uncle, Moses Polock, from whom he inherited his reluctance to sell a book. Then Sessler, in the person of Mabel Zahn, secured another edition for me, and the J. B. Lippincott Company, who are still printing and selling the book, sold me a copy for a dollar and a half; and still, like Oliver Twist, I asked for MORE. The "Cherry Tree" edition was the one I longed for—and I am likely to keep on longing. In the Bulletin of the New York Public Library for April 1932, one reads: "The first edition to contain the story of the hatchet and the cherry tree is the edition of 1806: the copy exhibited is the only one known." Now, while I was in the midst of this Weems fever I was called to the telephone one evening by my son, who told me to get myself into a dinner jacket and walk across the lawn to meet a very handsome woman at dinner, a Mrs. Virginia White of Cleveland. Rather reluctantly I left my desk and presently found myself seated by a woman whose charms had not been overstated. In the course of conversation she inquired if I was writing anything. "No," I replied, "nothing much; just at the moment I am amusing myself with Weems's *Life of Washington*; I don't suppose you have ever heard of the book."

"I know the book very well," replied the lady; "I have a copy of the Cherry Tree edition."

I looked at the lady, pityingly. "Madam," I said, "there is only one copy known of that edition: it is in the New York Public Library." Whereupon she smiled and said: "There was only one copy known until I discovered mine. The New York Library edition is cut; my copy is uncut and unopened." It is not often that a pretty woman at a dinner party is able to set me right about a book, and I ventured to express my doubts. Whereupon Mrs. White told the following story.

She had been born on a plantation in South Carolina; her hand had been sought in marriage (often, no doubt, but she did not tell me this) by a man living in Cleveland. On one occasion, going to her old home she found in an outbuilding a basket of old pamphlets which a gardener was about to consign to the flames. "Let me look them over first," said the lady; she did so, found and preserved the pamphlet. Instead of having it neatly bound and trimmed, as the average woman, or man, would have done, she took it to the New York Public Library and showed it to one of the librarians, who admitted that never before had he seen such a copy and told her to have a morocco case made for it. If I cared to examine it, my newly made friend would lend it to me. And so, here and now, on my writing table at the moment of writing is a copy of one of the rarest, and certainly the most amusing item of Americana in existence, in pristine condition. With it are some newspaper clippings and magazine articles about the famous book: one item especially attracted my attention. It seems that in some institution in the Middle West there is an iron casting of a hatchet some eighteen inches long, which the donor seemed to think proved that the cherry-tree legend was known before the time of Washington's death. Of course it does nothing of the kind. Weems said that he invented the story to teach American boys the importance of telling the truth. But Weems's word goes for nothing; he was a myth-maker, a liar after the order of Baron Munchausen. The pamphlet is nine by six inches, is in gray paper wrappers, and was reprinted, the title-page goes on to explain, by Geo. Randolph of Augusta (Georgia) in 1806 and is copyrighted—Weems does not say where or how. Copyrighted or not, the work will live when that of substantial historians is forgotten.

Feeling myself in Weemish mood, I observe that the hatchet in the western institution is not the original Washington hatchet, search for which still continues, but the hatchet of the late Carrie Nation, with which a generation ago that lady was wont to smash mirrors in barrooms, in a mistaken effort to bring about prohibition; as such it is a

Nation-al possession (Do I hear hisses?), and should be sent to the Smithsonian Institution in Washington to be forever preserved; like the apple which was shot, centuries ago, from the head of young William Tell, which is reverently preserved in the Museum at Berne. It is said that an old darky who lived on the Mount Vernon estate long after Washington's death was asked if he had seen young Master George hack his father's favorite cherry tree. "No sir, no sir," was his reply, "I didn't zackly see him hack it, sir, but I druv the hack." But let us be serious. We are discussing the first Life ever written of the Father of his Country, by Mason Locke Weems. It is not easy to interest me in clergymen, but Parson Weems, as he is always called, is in a class by himself. He was born in Maryland in 1759 and at an early age went to England to study medicine; tiring of this science he went abroad again and was regularly ordained an Episcopal clergyman; subsequently he became a schoolmaster, and finally a peddler of books and of medicine. No man was his superior in the gift of gab. He could lead, in the style of the late Billy Sunday, sinners to the Mercy Seat, or, with the predatory instincts of a peddler, at the tail of a cart dispose of a bottle of "Elixir of Life," for the trifling sum of sixty-two and a half cents; guaranteed to cure colds, coughs, and consumption, remove superfluous fat, develop the bust, curl straight hair, take the kink out of curly hair—and remove corns.

Merging his trades, he added to them that of biographer. He had now found his proper niche in the world. Of biographies he wrote several, but his *Life of Washington* was the first of over five hundred. The bibliography of Weems's masterpiece—for it is no less—is obscure. The first edition seems to have been published in 1800, a few weeks after Washington's death. I have never seen a perfect copy; I understand there is one in the Library of Congress, and there is a whole run of them in the Historical Society of Pennsylvania. His pamphlet—for originally it was no more—was printed anywhere and everywhere, as needed. It did not become thoroughly established as a book until Mathew Carey, the founder of the firm which a hundred years later became Lea & Febiger, took it up. The Lippincott edition is a substantial 12mo, and the most highfalutin, amusing book ever published. I wish every person in this auditorium would at once buy a copy and in so doing mention my name, for with taxes being what they are, us authors, as Mark Twain once wrote to Queen Victoria, are in for a hard winter. Weems, a peddler, a parson, and a physician, was, like Edison, an inventor. His invention was the story of the cherry tree. "Father, I cannot tell a lie, I did it with my little hatchet." There seems to have been an Episcopal clergyman by the name of Weems, one time rector of a church down in Virginia that Washington attended; it was too much to expect that book-peddler Weems would not attempt, and successfully, to pass himself as Rector Weems. He told intimate and personal stories of Washington and his Lady, so often that he came to believe them himself; stories grow that way. Out of a rather social, genial, fond-of-dancing, card-playing, horse-loving, fox-hunting human being, he manufactured a sanctimonious wooden image, which Washington remains for many of us in spite of the efforts of scholars to efface this idea. This is how he tells of Washington's death. With the resignation of a soldier he behaved like a Christian: "I am dying," he said to his physicians, "but I am not afraid to die." They sat around his bedside as he lay panting for breath; then they went out and the great man, feeling that the silver cord was loosing, closed his eyes with his own hands for the last time and fell asleep. Swift on angels' wings the brightening saint ascended while voices, more than human, warbled and hymned the procession towards the heavenly gate, from which myriads of angels hastened forth with golden harps. High in front was seen the beauteous form of Franklin, his cheeks of celestial rosy red; his robe, like a morning cloud, streaked with gold, a heavenly star glittering on his forehead. Angels poured around in transports of unutterable tenderness to meet their Washington and embrace him, while tears of joy, such as only angels weep, rolled down their rosy cheeks.

But let us be serious. What would Dr. Rosenbach say if he could hear us? Let us speak of Benjamin Franklin—not the rosy red angel carrying a harp and wearing a star upon his forehead, but that very sedate old gentleman in homespun the color of cold gravy, whose *Autobiography* presents one of the prettiest bibliographical puzzles I know. I bought a copy of the first English edition only a few weeks ago from a bookseller's catalogue. For the details which follow I am largely indebted to my friend and neighbor, Mr. Franklin Bache, his grandson several times removed. The *Autobiography* was written at four different times: the first and most interesting portion when the great man was a house guest of Dr. Jonathan Shipley, the Bishop of St. Asaph, Twyford, England, in 1771; when he returned to Philadelphia in 1775 he brought the manuscript with him. He took up the subject nine years later when residing at

Passy, near Paris, and wrote a second portion, and a third portion was written in Philadelphia in 1788, the last few pages in the same place shortly before his death in 1790.

According to Paul Leicester Ford, Franklin's bibliographer, there were six or eight more or less complete copies of the manuscript in existence when Franklin died. So much is reasonably clear; it is only when one begins to deal with the printed book, or rather books, that the fun begins.

The first part was addressed to his son and was not intended for publication, but the work probably had some circulation in manuscript in Paris during Franklin's long residence there. Certain it is, however, that someone, no one knows who, made a translation of it, the first part, into French and it was published in Paris by Buisson in 1791. Franklin, dead by now, had been enormously popular in France, as why, with his great variety of gifts, should he not have been? By this time the manuscript had disappeared; what more natural than that a translation into English should be made? So a great book, indeed our greatest classic, written originally in English, was translated into French and translated back into English but it did not appear in our language until 1793, when two different London editions appeared; one edition in a single volume for J. Parsons, and the other in two volumes for G. and J. Robinson, both having shops in Paternoster Row. The two editions could hardly have appeared on the same day: which is the earlier? no one knows, positively; perhaps the records of the Stationers' Hall in London would show. In any event, the *Autobiography* was thus launched and on its glorious way; it was translated into perhaps a dozen languages, and quite recently Mr. Bache found a little edition printed in German at Ephrata in 1796. It had the stamp of the University of Pennsylvania in it, and was returned to our Library whence it had strayed or been stolen. Then there was the publication of the second part, in French also, with the first, in Paris in 1798. The third part was not included in any edition until William Temple Franklin published it in London in 1818, and the fourth part was not published until ten years later when it too appeared in French. Few books have so curious a record; where are all these various manuscripts? Only one is known to exist, that which was formerly the property of John Bigelow, who edited and published it. This is the edition which one usually finds in libraries. The manuscript is now in the Henry E. Huntington Library at San Gabriel, California; I have held it in my hand but have not examined it, for when I saw it Mr. Huntington had just acquired it and was so enthusiastic over it that I could but listen to him. I remember that he told me that its possession gave him a greater thrill than anything in his library. I have read the book only once, many years ago, and it would be impertinent for me to praise what has been so universally admired. Franklin is *sui generis*, no one reminds us of him; the ablest diplomat of his time, he was also the greatest philosopher —use this last word how you will. How he could have lived for so many years in London, a friend of Strahan, the printer, without having met Dr. Johnson, also an intimate friend of Strahan's, I cannot say; but meet they did not, or the crash of an irresistible force meeting with an immovable body would have left its repercussions to the present day.

And all this mess of words is the result of coming quite unexpectedly upon an item in a recent Rosenbach catalogue, offering for sale a fine uncut copy of the first London edition, a book I have always wanted. It is now in the "Oak Knoll" Library and I bethink me of the text, Proverbs xx: 14, which Dr. Rosenbach frequently appends to those catalogues which are the despair of bibliophiles:

> It is naught, it is naught,
> saith the buyer: but when he is
> gone his way, then he boasteth.

I seem to remember something about the devil quoting Scripture upon occasion.

I have so many sale catalogues that it is difficult to make a selection. Many, if not most of the sales took place soon after the deaths of the men who made the collections; the question arises:

> Seeing how soon that I was done for,
> I wonder why I was begun for.

I have seen these lines on a tombstone of a child in an English country churchyard. Let me attempt to answer the question. Generally a man begins to buy books because he likes to read, then he buys books that he can never hope to read, and the taste grows by what it feeds on. Presently the man finds that he has the nucleus of a library, and he begins to fill in. Perhaps he has by now chosen an author, or a subject, or a period. When one throws a stone into a lake it disappears but it leaves a circle, an ever enlarging circle; so with book collecting, and then like the stone the man disappears, but the books that he has assembled with so much care remain to tell what manner of man he was, but too often not for long—especially today. Frequently libraries have passed undisturbed from one generation to another, or perhaps they were bequeathed to some existing library, or if the collection was sufficiently important it became the Bodleian in Oxford, or the Morgan in New York, or the Huntington in California, or the Folger in Washington —named after the donors—and scholars generally are not sufficiently appreciative of what these great collectors have done for them. Had there not first been collectors, there would hardly have been scholars worthy of the name. I am thinking of the library of Mr. George Arents, Jr. of New York. His library contains every known volume in which the word "tobacco," historically used, appears, but look at his catalogue upon which his librarian, Jerome E. Brooks, has been at work for several years. The subject takes us far afield. I am thinking also of the library of my friend Mr. Carl H. Pforzheimer, also of New York, and of the accomplished young scholar, Mr. William A. Jackson, who is at this moment at work upon the catalogue of it. It will fill three large volumes, English Literature to the year 1740, and I make the prediction that never before has there been made so full and accurate a catalogue as that to which Mr. Jackson is now giving his untiring attention. Shall this library be Mr. Pforzheimer's monument? Shall he need another? "Yes" to the first question—"No" to the second.

But too often our libraries disappear with us—like the stone in the lake, they cause a ripple at the time, that is all. It is inevitable that small collections be dispersed, but a feeling of sadness overcomes one as one thinks of a man spending freely of his time, his money, and his energy, and ere he is cold in his grave enter his executors with power to act and sell under the hammer of the auctioneer the books which were once part and parcel of the man himself. Certainly the disposal of a man's library should be undertaken as reverently as the disposal of his "corps," which in some sort his library is. I am thinking of another, not library, but a collection of books which should never be disseverated. (It is Gabriel Wells's word.) I refer to Mr. Ellis Ames Ballard's Kipling Collection. A man of my own age or a trifle better—or worse—Mr. Ballard has gone about his collecting with the fine frenzy of the lunatic, the lover, and the poet. Show Ballard a Walton's *Angler* in an original binding and he tells you he is a farmer, not a fisherman; show him a *Comus*, as I once did, and it leaves him cold; but show him an uncut copy of Kipling's *Departmental Ditties* of relatively little value, as I am able to do, and he looks despondent, but only for a split second. I am warned by a common friend that if I call his beautifully printed volume on Kipling a catalogue I shall not receive a copy but I shall take a chance, for Ballard is one of the kindest and most generous of men; and we have been friends half a century.

If Chauncey Brewster Tinker, Professor of English and Keeper of the Rare Books in the Library at Yale, would publish a catalogue of his personal and private collection of rare books, other professors of English would either kill him or commit suicide; perhaps I should not so much as hint that in his profession he has no rival as a collector. If he blames me, as I am told that he does, for his becoming distinguished as a collector, let me tell him that when all his admiring pupils are dead and he himself is by way of being forgotten, his library will remain as an evidence of what learning and persistence will do in a game which is too often regarded as the sport of the very rich.

It is only a step from Tinker to the *Catalogue of Books*,

Manuscripts and Prints relating to Dr. Samuel Johnson and his Era, in the library of Mr. R. B. Adam of Buffalo, New York. This work fills three portly volumes and is the work of its owner, a busy man and a merchant as well as a scholar. It was an honor I greatly appreciated when, with Professors Osgood, of Princeton, and Tinker, I was asked to write an Introduction to this important work. Mr. Adam's Johnson Collection is, like Colonel Isham's Boswell, the despair of his rivals. Where other Johnson collectors have a dozen or so of items which we prize, and justly, they have hundreds. The Adam collection has been more than half a century a-forming, having been begun by Mr. Adam's uncle from whom he inherited the nucleus years ago. Birkbeck Hill, the great editor of Boswell, fifty years ago spoke of the Adam collection in Buffalo, on the shore of Lake Erie, as being without equal in England, and it has been its owner's pleasure constantly to add to it.

Into how small a space can I compress a reference to the famous Boswell Catalogue of Colonel Isham? This is one of the outstanding romances of modern collecting. The story goes—I should say, went—that after the death of Boswell the material which entered largely into his great Biography of Johnson had been burnt: so the story was told for more than a century; a few years ago rumors reached this country that it was safe in the keeping of a scion of the Boswell line in Malahide Castle in Ireland. How it got there need not concern us; the fact is that it was there and that after much negotiation it was purchased *en bloc* by Colonel Isham and brought to this country, where it was edited and published in part by Geoffrey Scott, and upon his death the work was taken up and completed by Professor Pottle of

Yale, a disciple of Professor Tinker. The whole work is available—except for an Index which is now in preparation —in eighteen magnificent volumes designed by Bruce Rogers and sumptuously printed, with facsimiles, so perfect that they can hardly be told from the originals, by Rudge. The price of the work is, if I remember, nine hundred dollars, which might be thought excessive did we not know that the cost by far exceeded the selling price. With this collection and this publication Isham writes his name forever among the great collectors of our time.

The first outstanding auction sale of books in this country was that of George Brinley, of Hartford, Connecticut. The dispersal of this great library was spread over several years; the first part was sold in 1879. It was a library largely of Americana, and the whole collection realized about one hundred and thirty thousand dollars. The most important item in the sale was a fine Gutenberg Bible. It would be interesting and possible to follow the progress of this great book from sale to sale and from place to place, but it would be I think more interesting to refer to the correspondence between Mr. Brinley and his agent in London, Henry Stevens of Vermont, as he always signed himself. To do so I shall not refer to the letters themselves but to excerpts from them which I published some years ago in an essay in which I called the Bible the greatest book in the world, a title which has never been challenged. It was from James Lenox, of New York, that in 1847 the same Henry Stevens received instructions to buy a Gutenberg Bible, no limit being fixed. When informed that the price paid was five hundred dollars, Mr. Lenox was tempted to repudiate the transaction, but he thought better of it and lived to congratulate himself on his purchase; the book is now in the New York Public Library.

Twenty-five years later a second Gutenberg Bible crossed the Atlantic, Mr. Brinley being the purchaser. Two noble lords wanted the book, but ready money was necessary; there was an exchange of letters, then of cables, with the result that Stevens secured the book and dispatched it, "insured against all risques," to its new owner, with this note of comment:

Pray, sir, ponder for a moment and appreciate the rarity and importance of this precious consignment from the Old World to the New. Not only is it the first Bible, but it is the first book ever printed. It was read in Europe half a century before America was discovered. Please suggest to your deputy that he uncover his head while in the presence of this great book. Let no custom house official or other man, in or out of authority, see it without first reverently raising his hat. It is not possible for many men ever to touch or even look upon a page of a Gutenberg Bible.

At the present time forty-five copies of the Gutenberg Bible are known, most of them lodged in public libraries from which they will never emerge. Mr. Pforzheimer has one; so has Mr. Joseph E. Widener of this city. Even fragments, single leaves, are of value; the highest price known to have been paid for a leaf, with an introduction by your orator, is six hundred and fifty dollars. When the George Brinley copy was sold at auction, in 1881, it made, as the saying is, eight thousand dollars. Hamilton Cole paid this price and later sold it to Brayton Ives for sixteen thousand. It was sold at the Ives Sale in 1891 for fourteen thousand eight hundred, being bought by James W. Ellsworth, then of Chicago, who sold it privately to Dr. Rosenbach, who sold it to its present owner, John H. Schiede of Titusville, Pennsylvania, for a price unknown. The Morgan Library in New York has no less than three copies, one on vellum and two on paper. The copy in the Library of Congress was secured from Dr. Otto Vollbehr of Berlin, who is said to have paid over three hundred thousand dollars for it, but this, I feel sure, like other fantastic figures coming from Washington, is a dream.

The greatest book sale I ever attended, the greatest library ever sold in this country, was that of Robert Hoe. It was twenty-five years ago and Dr. Rosenbach had not yet come into prominence; George D. Smith, representing Mr. Huntington—then just getting into his stride—carried off the honors; he—or should I say they?—bought against all comers. The sale was held at Anderson's; I well remember the applause when Mr. Huntington bought the Gutenberg Bible, on vellum, for fifty thousand dollars—a mad price it was said at the time; book collectors are always paying mad prices and seeing them go madder still. Dr. Rosenbach paid one hundred and six thousand dollars some years later for a copy which Mrs. Edward S. Harkness took off his hands almost before the hammer fell and gave to Yale. The catalogue of the Hoe Sale in ten volumes is a book of reference to be found in every good bibliographical library—and in some that are not so good, my own for example.

Great enjoyment can be had in reading the catalogues of small private collections, and among these the catalogue entitled *A Sentimental Library*, formed by the late Harry B. Smith, is one of the most delightful. I insert the word "late," for Mr. Smith died while I was writing this paper. He was the author of the book of *Robin Hood* set to delicious music by Reginald De Koven, undoubtedly the most successful of our indigenous comic operas. Harry Smith was a real book lover. One is asked frequently, "Do book collectors know their books?" The answer is, "It all depends." Mr. Morgan was the greatest book collector this country has ever had; his knowledge of his library was far greater than was the knowledge of Mr. Huntington of his, but it was not, it could not have been the detailed, personal knowledge of the collector of a few hundred or even a few thousand choice books, every one of which he knows more or less intimately. Some men know books as they know lords, by name, and then boast of their acquaintance. And remember that it has been said that

> Unlearned men of books assume the care,
> As eunuchs are the guardians of the fair.

The subtitle of Harry Smith's catalogue is "Comprising books formerly owned by famous writers, presentation copies, manuscripts and drawings." Does not this suggest a feast? Is not the title, *A Sentimental Library*, well chosen? It describes my library as well as his. The whole Sentimental Library passed one day into the temporary keeping of Dr. Rosenbach and was placed on sale by him the day the *Lusitania* was sunk during the Great War. The fact that we were all scared to death that day prevented my buying as much as I should have done, but some of the most interesting books in my library are "Sentimental" items.

Catalogues serve another excellent purpose; by means of them one can trace valuable books from library to library with as much certainty as one can trace the pedigree of a famous horse. And men especially learned in what we collectors call "provenance"—that is, the whenceabouts of books—can tell at a glance the library or libraries from which a book has come. Especially skilled in this art are Seymour de Ricci of Paris, and William A. Jackson of New York; their knowledge—or should it be called a sixth sense —is positively uncanny: without opening a book either of these men will say, "Oh, I see you've got the Hoe-Hagen-Chew copy of *Paradise Lost*. I wondered what had become of it."

This may be as good a place as any to call attention to the difference between a bookseller, a stationer, a printer, a binder, and a publisher, yet all these trades frequently have been merged into one. A bookseller must have a stock of books if he wishes to survive—if you don't believe it, ask Dr. Rosenbach. A stationer, too, must have a shop in which he sells paper, pens, ink, etc. A printer must have types, presses, etc.; and a binder pasteboard, leather, and tools. But a publisher requires none of these things: he can start a business using the other fellow's plant and the author's brains—and he frequently asks him to put up some money too. The Brontë girls advanced their publishers, Aylott and Jones, thirty-odd guineas and a further sum for advertising when they published their slender little volume of *Poems* by Currer, Ellis, and Acton Bell. After a year, when they asked for an accounting they were told that just *two* copies had been sold; such copies as have since come upon the market were given away by the sisters as presents. Need I say that the book with the Aylott and Jones title-page is exceedingly rare?

Thomas Hardy advanced his first publisher, Tinsley—old Tinsley he is usually called—seventy-five pounds towards the cost of the publication of *Desperate Remedies*. I have the original letter in which the terms are stated. But perhaps most interesting of all is the story of the publication of *Wuthering Heights*, by Emily, and *Agnes Grey* by Anne Brontë. The publisher, Thomas Cautley Newby, extracted fifty pounds from the two girls, and they never received from him a penny, not even an accounting. In the same year, the same publisher brought out Trollope's first book, *The Macdermots of Ballycloran*; he wisely put up no money and he received none; likewise no accounting. Here then is a coincidence; two of the rarest, practically unobtainable novels of the mid-Victorian period were published in the same year, 1847, by the same rascally publisher who would certainly turn in his grave could he be told that a copy of either of these novels would fetch today, in good condition—shall we say a thousand pounds? Pounds, not dollars, mind you. With these facts before us we can easily understand Byron's famous rearrangement of the text. John xviii: 40, "Now Barabbas was a publisher."

I wish I could ask you to look over my shoulder while I examine the sale catalogue of the late and not too Reverend Laurence Sterne, of which only one copy seems to have survived to be reproduced in facsimile by my friend Hugh Tregaskis, the well-known London bookseller. It is a slender volume with an introduction by Charles Whibley, from which I make the following notes. Sterne died in 1768 and his books were sold *en bloc* to Todd & Southeran, Booksellers at the Sign of the Golden Bible in the cathedral city of York. They paid eighty pounds for the lot, only twenty

pounds more than was paid for his carriage and pair. A catalogue was made and the books we are assured "are to be
sold exceedingly cheap": they were. Prices were affixed to
most items, but the catalogue begins with Caxton's *Game
and Play of Chess*, lacking the title-page. Did not the booksellers know that it never had any? Books had colophons in
those days, but they add a note: "This book is generally
allowed by all the typographical antiquaries to have been
the first specimen of the art among us." What did they sell
it for? and where is it now?—an echo answers "What" and
"Where?" Would twenty thousand dollars be too much?
Dr. Rosenbach, an authority, thinks it would be a gift at
that price. There is a *Gulliver's Travels*, first edition, 1726,
neat—"neat" mark you!—for three shillings! Oh my God,
this is too harrowing! and a folio Beaumont and Fletcher
for six. There was good old Burton, his *Anatomy of Melancholy*, for eighteen pence, of which it is usual for the cata-
loguers of these days to say that "Johnson praised it, Carlyle pummeled it, and Sterne pillaged it"—as indeed he did.
Dr. Johnson's *Dictionary* was lacking, but his translation of
Father Lobo's *Voyage to Abyssinia* was to be had for three
shillings. And all these were association volumes, for were
they not Yorick's, alas! poor Yorick—and not so poor neither, for with his flashes of wit and wisdom has he not cheated
Father Time, that old gentleman who has a wallet at his
back wherein he puts alms for oblivion? I think so. We
hardly needed this catalogue to discover the books Sterne
"pillaged"—he took his good where he found it and was
unashamed, but the best of Sterne was his own; was he not
the creator of my Uncle Toby and Mr. Shandy, and does
not his "God tempers the wind to the shorn lamb" sound

like a bit from the Bible? And now I remember that he
pilfered this too. Ah well, shall we look upon his like again?
I am inclined to doubt it.

Next to Sterne's Catalogue is a slender and valuable little book I acquired more than ten years ago in London, the
*Sale Catalogue of the Valuable Library of Books of theLate
Learned Samuel Johnson, Esquire, LL.D., Deceased*—as the
title-page informs us—and subsequently I discovered that
it had once been General Oglethorpe's, the founder of the
State of Georgia. Samuel Rogers, the Banker Poet who attended the sale, is quoted as saying, "I met General Oglethorpe at the sale of Dr. Johnson's books; he was then
eighty-eight: his face looked like parchment." I wonder if
the General knew that Samuel Ireland was making a sketch
of him at the sale, in a full-bottom wig, with a three-corner
hat, holding my identical Catalogue in his hand? I have a
reproduction of it. The sale took place at Christie's Great
Room, in Pall Mall, on Wednesday, February 16th, 1785,
and the three following days. Let us look at some of the
books the Doctor had and see what they fetched. There
were six hundred and fifty lots, and they brought in all two
hundred and thirty-two pounds, seventeen shillings, including a number of framed and glazed portraits: these sold in
lots of four, eight, and ten, though some, perhaps many,
were after Reynolds' pictures and quite likely were the gift
of the artist himself. We know that the sale was largely attended, many people desiring to buy a book that had once
belonged to the famous man. Remember, too, that these
were the great Lexicographer's tools; some have lost their
cutting edge by now, yet they once served so powerful and
rugged an intellect that it made its way against such ob-

stacles as humble birth, poverty, disease, and neglect, until finally its possessor came to be honored of all men and we now speak of his age as being the "Age of Johnson"—what a triumph!

In glancing over the items that made up the sale, one is struck by the number of books in Latin and in Greek. Perhaps this is not so remarkable as is the absence of books by his literary friends and acquaintance; I account for this by the fact that many lots were called "bundles," "parcels," "large bundles," "a large quantity of pamphlets in a box" sold for one pound, eleven and six; perhaps these were not thought worth binding when they were received as gifts. What would one say to a presentation pamphlet of *She Stoops to Conquer* or a *Deserted Village*? What became of the little volume in which the Doctor had written, "This was dear Tetty's book"—Tetty being his nickname for his wife—and what was the condition of his First Folio of Shakespeare that it brought only one pound two shillings? Doubtless it was imperfect; perhaps it was disfigured by its owner's own notes. What would not one give to own it? Today a single leaf of this great book has value, and a First Folio used by the great man when he was, tardily, editing his edition of Shakespeare! . . . The mere idea staggers one's imagination. Was the Burton's *Anatomy of Melancholy* the identical copy that served as an alarm clock to get the Doctor out of bed two hours before he wished to rise? We note that Johnson kept up his interest in "Chymistry" to the last; he had an up-to-date dictionary on the subject; and just before he died he bought or had given him a new Greek Testament. Medicine, too, kept his attention: he had *Mudge on Coughs* and *James on Fevers*. He had Goldsmith's

Roman History, but where is his *Vicar of Wakefield*? Dear Mrs. Carter's *Epictetus* is here, and one remembers Johnson's remark: "My old friend Mrs. Carter could make a pudding as well as translate *Epictetus*"; also: "A man is in general better pleased when he has a good dinner on his table than when his wife talks Greek." Here is Boswell's *Corsica*, of which subject Johnson once told Bozzy to "empty his head." And Johnson's own *Dictionary* with notes in his own hand, for thirteen shillings. But why call the tantalizing roll? It is to be remembered, however, that shillings were not as plentiful in 1785 as dollars are today; they are making money very fast in Washington.

Compared with Dr. Johnson's sale, that of Mrs. Thrale-Piozzi, which took place on Wednesday, May 8th, 1816, is of little interest. The sale took place at her mansion at Streatham, the lady at the time being at her Tremeirchion home in Wales, whither, I think, her best books had been taken. Johnson was represented by his Shakespeare in eight volumes and a presentation copy of his *Dictionary*, which is now mine; for the rest, there were books in Latin and Greek, French and Italian, for the lady was no mean scholar. Of what society woman of the present day could this be said?

The most amazing of the little cluster of sale catalogues before me is, undoubtedly, that of the Honorable Topham Beauclerk, amazing because of its range and the character of the man who put the library together. Is it necessary for me to tell you that he was the great grandson of Charles II out of Nell Gwyn, as the stud books say; that he was an intimate friend of Dr. Johnson, although thirty years younger than he; rich, brilliant, and dissipated, yet withal a scholar? It was Beauclerk who, along with Bennet Langton, another scholarly lad, routed Dr. Johnson out of his bed one night, past midnight, to go on a "frisk" with them, and a frisk it was. "What a coalition!" exclaimed Garrick when he heard of this gay party, "soon I shall be having to bail my old friend out of the Round-house." But Johnson was never content to let the other man have the last word. "Ah," said Johnson, "Garrick would have gone but his wife wouldn't let him." But the item at which I wish to arrive is *The Pithy, Pleasant and Profitable Workes*, by Master Skelton, Poet Laureate to King Henry VIII, now collected and newly published, Anno. 1568. This brought seventeen shillings and six pence. I boast a copy; it is one of the rarest little volumes in English literature: its cost is a profound secret. Beauclerk lived—and his house still stands—in Great Russell Street. It housed a library of thirty thousand volumes in all languages, which was dispersed after his death, in 1781. The sale continued for fifty days; a priced copy of the catalogue, desperately rare and almost worthless, is before me. It is a large volume of 368 pages; the books are grouped in their various languages, then according to size, then alphabetically, with exasperating variations. Turning to the English section we find such authors as Fielding, Sterne, and Johnson, Goldsmith and the rest, but the prices! they positively make one faint. Here is Goldsmith's *Vicar*, first edition, for four and six, and Johnson's *Prince of Abyssinia*, first edition, for six shillings, and his *Poets*, four volumes in fine morocco, for one pound, three. He had Johnson's *Dictionary*, of course, and a copy of the *Plan*, but I forget what they fetched. *Tristam Shandy* lumped with the *Sentimental Journey* brought sixteen shillings. Beauclerk's wife was Lady Diana, a peeress in her own right, the eldest daughter of the Second Duke of Marlborough. She was not true to him; perhaps it was too much to expect that she should have been: in any event, Johnsonians will remember the very coarse name he applied to her—the famous passage in Boswell could hardly have been her favorite reading; indeed it may be doubted that she cared for the biography at all; many people did not; it was said that Boswell had invented a new kind of libel.

With the Kern Sale in New York in 1929, the curtain fell upon an era. We know now that we then were mad. The Republican Party through its representatives was about to *abolish poverty*. Bankers were preparing to send New York Central stock to two hundred and fifty dollars a share and *keep it there*. What more natural than that books worth hundreds should have brought thousands. A fine uncut copy of *Tom Jones* brought twenty-nine thousand dollars! How well I remember getting a copy of the Paris *New York Herald* up the Nile, at Luxor, one morning, and reading a detailed account of the sale; I knew then that my book-collecting days were over: the market had been taken away from the likes o' me. I had left a few bids; I got one book and, thank God, only one.

My mind goes back twenty years, to earlier and to better days when the last of the founders of the Grolier Club were in the saddle, men like Mr. Halsey and Beverly Chew; how after the auction sales we would meet at the Plaza for a little supper and fight our battles over again. Shall those days come again? Of course they will, but like the fireworks in *The Mikado*, I shall not see them—but they will be here all the same. I hate to think of an important sale—my own for example—which I shall not be able to attend, catalogue and pencil in hand. Rather let me recall one night at Anderson's, years ago, when a passionate love letter from John Keats to Fanny Brawne was sold. May I suggest the auction room crowded with men and women in evening dress? Upon a platform stood a red velvet altar, on either side were red velvet curtains partly drawn. Concealed electric light played upon a tiny sheet of paper displayed upon the altar. Kit Morley, the ever accomplished and versatile Kit, made it the subject of a sonnet; it is brilliantly written. I shall read it to you from a manuscript copy. Remember there are two persons speaking: the auctioneer and the poet.

In an Auction Room

(Letter of John Keats to Fanny Brawne,
Anderson Galleries, March 15, 1920

How about this lot? said the auctioneer;
One hundred, may I say, just for a start?
Between the plum-red curtains, drawn apart,
A written sheet was held.... And strange to hear
(Dealer, would I were steadfast as thou art)
The cold quick bids. (_Against you in the rear!_)
The crimson salon, in a glow more clear
Burned bloodlike purple as the poet's heart.

Song that outgrew the singer! Bitter Love
That broke the proud hot heart it held in thrall —
Poor script, where still those tragic passions move —
Eight hundred bid: fair warning: the last call:
The soul of Adonais, like a star.....
Sold for eight hundred dollars — Doctor R!

III. Essays *and* Essayists

WHEN I sat down at my desk to consider what I should say on this, the last time I shall address you, I sought a subject that would permit me to wander, as my habit is, and I pitched upon the Essay as affording me scope enough. For the Essay is like a stagecoach; however crowded, there is usually room for one more. "Are you full inside?" asked a man approaching a stagecoach which was about to set out on a journey. "I am, very full," said a man, sticking his head out of the window—the man's name was Charles Lamb. On the whole, I feel that the subject I have chosen will suit me admirably—I hope that it may suit you. Let us begin.

Historically, the essay is a newcomer in literature; both the word and the thing are only older than the novel by a century or two. It was the discovery of Michel de Montaigne, a wise and tolerant Frenchman, who was born in Périgord in 1533, died in 1592, an especially intolerant period: he was about forty at the time of the Massacre of St. Bartholomew. (Agnes Repplier tells me that, as a child, she often wondered who massacred him!) Perhaps I should say that the essay was his invention; certainly he gave it a name. The world had three very great writers at about that period: England had Shakespeare, the greatest of all, who died April 23rd, 1616; Spain had Cervantes, who died on the same day in the same year, an amazing coincidence; and France had Montaigne, who had died thirty-odd years before; certainly it is fair to speak of these three men as contemporaries. Kipling has a set of pretty verses about Shakespeare and Miguel of Spain standing at the top of the stair in Paradise to welcome Jane—Austen, of course—and we may, if we like, think of Shakespeare and Cervantes ascending the stair, side by side, to be met at the top by Montaigne holding out a hand of welcome to each.

Montaigne's *Essais* were first published in Bordeaux, in 1580, in two octavo volumes; two years later a second edition was published, and five years later a third; in each of these editions there were some changes and additions. The fourth edition, published in 1588 at Paris, was the last edition to be published during its author's lifetime; in 1595 appeared the first posthumous edition, and this is the edition which John Florio chose as the one to be "Englished." It is usual to speak of Florio's Montaigne as having a freedom and fluency that is often called "Elizabethan," but scholars are generally of the opinion that a later translation, that of Charles Cotton, published in 1685, is closer but less racy. How should I know? My own Montaigne library is a slender one; I have a first Florio edition, a small folio, "unwashed," as the catalogues say, bound in its original vellum, and it pleases me to remember that the first book I ever bought from Dr. Rosenbach, when he was just setting out on his distinguished career as a bookseller, was the Cotton edition, also bound in vellum, edited by the rather cantankerous William Carew Hazlitt, the author of *Four Generations of a Literary Family*, the first edition of which was suppressed, for an excellent reason. I have also the trans-

lation of George B. Ives, published some ten years ago by
the Harvard University Press. My actual and very slight
acquaintance with Montaigne began thirty years ago with a
brief but charming biography of the essayist by Edward
Dowden; I read it with delight when it first appeared, and I
have read it since. Dowden was an Irishman who knew literature well; he was a good scholar, and had a fine Montaigne collection; unluckily, he is especially remembered for
a silly whitewashing Life of Shelley; Mark Twain gave it a
terrific slating. The book, however, which led me back to
Montaigne and is in some measure responsible for this lecture, is the so-called *Autobiography*, by Marvin Lowenthal,
published about a year ago by Houghton Mifflin & Co.;
this volume is a sheer delight. In it Montaigne lives, for
English readers, as he has hardly lived before. Mr. Lowenthal has assembled and very largely translated much, if not
all that Montaigne says about himself, and no one, not even
Rousseau, ever wrote more freely and frankly of himself
than did the author of the *Essais*. And as Rousseau was
mean and contemptible and rather gloried in it, Montaigne,
although he did not hesitate to paint his warts, could hardly
conceal the fact that he was generous and benign in mood,
when he sat down to meditate and to write. It was Carl Van
Doren who recommended the publication of this remarkable book to the publishers, to whom he wrote as follows:
"This manuscript brings an undying book to new life"—
and much more. It certainly does. The full title of the book
is *The Autobiography of Michel de Montaigne*, "comprising
the life of the wisest man of his time: his childhood, youth
and prime; his adventures in love and marriage, at court,
and in office, war, revolution and plague; his travels at home

and abroad; his habits, tastes, whims and opinions." Low-enthal adds, too, that "the whole has been selected, ar-ranged, edited, prefaced, and mostly translated anew from his Essays, etc. withholding no signal or curious detail." This is a large, a very large order, and admirably has our editor filled it. It was no less than a stroke of genius to take the long, tedious, and sometimes involved Essays and fit them for modern, busy, and I may add, mature readers so that the reader seems to be hearing and seeing the wise old gentleman, in shabby clothes and easy shoes, sit down be-fore his fire and have his talk out. Should my friend Dr. Francis Packard by any chance hear my voice, he will, I fear, cut my acquaintance. "Tedious? Man, you're mad!" he will exclaim. But it will be remembered that my knowl-edge of Montaigne is superficial, I am no scholar of any kind—Dr. Packard is, but I am giving this lecture, not he.

In France, Montaigne is regarded very much as we re-gard Shakespeare, although it seems that no two men could be more unlike. Our great dramatist and poet no doubt had his own personal opinions on the matters and things of his time, on matters and things of all time, but the opinions ex-pressed in the plays are invariably the opinions of the crea-tures of his imagination, not of himself. Shakespeare does not mention the Bible: we do not know whether he was a Catholic or a Protestant; we do know that he was for king and country, and no more brilliant and biting attack upon the functioning of democracy—that is to say, upon the mob —has ever been written than Act III, Scene 7, of *King Rich-ard III*. Toss this book aside and look it up. Montaigne, however, expresses his opinion freely, and he cares not a rap for any man's opinion but his own, and not very much

for that. His father, or perhaps it was his grandfather, purchased the right to a coat of arms; the son chose his, a bal-
ance of scales: his motto was QUI SCAI JE?—What do I
know? "This is what I think but I may be wrong; I probably am," he says. He is as self-centered as a tenor singing
a solo in a country church of an Easter Sunday while the
collection is being taken up, and as modest as a girl going
to her first communion. "The prince of egotists," Emerson
calls him; he also calls him a skeptic. Montaigne was an
enigma to himself. He thought he was a Catholic, but he
was accused of being a Protestant—when at Mass, as he
crossed himself, he yawned. He could not for the life of him
understand why both religions enjoyed the shedding of blood
under conditions which they strove to make as agonizing as
possible. In our time he would be called an agnostic, but
that useful word had not, in his day, been invented. By the
exercise of great skill he managed to keep on good terms
with rival kings, but he expected from time to time to have
his throat cut by one party or the other, or both together.
When civil war raged around him he said he did not despair: "Our government is very sick indeed but others have
been more so without dying." It might be well for us to remember this. When things were at their worst he did not
bolt the door of his chateau, anyone was free to enter; rivals
brought their papers and jewels to him for safe-keeping,
and he managed to die very comfortably—or rather I should
say uncomfortably—in his bed, for he suffered severely from
a painful disease, at the age of sixty; also he had the gout,
although it was his habit to drench his wine with water.
And he might well have said, and with better reason, as the
dying essayist Hazlitt did, "Well, I've had a happy life,"

for he was at all times comfortably off; he was honored by his King and adored by his fellow townsmen. When he went to Rome he was given the freedom of the great city: his citizenship was evidenced by a great diploma glorious in gilt lettering and seals. It pleased him greatly, but he knew it all to be vanity and that it would probably be followed by vexation—which it was, for while he was away he was elected Mayor of Bordeaux, then the third largest city in France. He had been taught to speak Latin before he spoke French, therefore he felt entirely at home in Rome. He did not want to be Mayor of Bordeaux, he preferred to lead the quiet life of a country gentleman with his books, but the King told him to take the job—he did, and made a good one. Learned, wise, witty, and full of curiosity; one thing, one man, he knew better than anyone else in the world—himself, and he told the story of himself in his *Essais* so delightfully and frankly that for three hundred and fifty years, generation after generation of readers of all nations turn to it with delight. In his *Autobiography*, as Lowenthal calls it, he says nothing about his mother; she may have died early: much about his father, whom he adored; his wife he seems to have regarded chiefly as the mother of his children—he had quite a crop, all girls; they died in infancy, except one, whom he mentions rather contemptuously as having, at twenty-three, no bust; but finally he got her married—that was a good job done.

We picture him a satisfied man among his books, reading and writing and forgetting. To be able to forget he thought was a blessing; it kept him from remembering his injuries, and it enabled him to read books he had read before and forgotten, and to read them with all the pleasure of novelty: this pleasure is not unknown to me. Some things from books he especially wanted to remember, that they might control his meditations; and to that end he had about fifty mottoes and maxims lettered on the rafters of his library in the tower. One, in Greek, translates: "No one has ever known the truth and no one ever will." Another, in Latin: "Enjoy pleasantly present things, others are beyond thee." His central thought, if I may so term it, was the well-known sentence of Terence, "I am a man, nothing human is alien to me," and well did he live up to it. His mottoes were taken from the Bible and from classical authors, and scholars have for centuries amused themselves in running down these quotations and seeing and debating to what extent they influenced his life and conduct. Montaigne was interested first in himself, then in his books: if he had thought of it he would have exclaimed with Caliban, in *The Tempest*: "Without books I am but a sot." Having books, he warmed both hands against the fire of life, and it is only by chance that he let a better man say:

>   We are such stuff
> As dreams are made on; and our little life
> Is rounded with a sleep.

It is now time for us to return to John Florio, the first translator of all this. His book was published in 1603 and at once became enormously popular among the most able and those that could but spell. It was dedicated in a long and tedious letter to a group of noble dames. If we may guess that Montaigne would have enjoyed Shakespeare, we know that the Dramatist read the Essayist, for he quotes a few lines—almost literally, as was his habit when he quoted at all—in *The Tempest*, where he makes Gonzalo say that in an ideal commonwealth there should be no kind of traffic, no name of magistrate; letters should not be known; riches, poverty, contract, succession, and occupation none; all men idle, and women too, but innocent and pure. All things in common nature should produce without sweat or endeavor. There is somewhat more, but turn we to the source of all this in the *Essais* where Montaigne says that in his (Montaigne's) Republic he would have no kind of traffic, no knowledge of letters, no name of magistrate, no service, riches, poverty, no succession, occupation, but all idle with no use of wine or corn or metal. I have quoted freely but I have not distorted; my wish is to place before you the Father of the Essay as he is.

John Florio, the first translator of Montaigne, as I have said, was the son of a Florentine Protestant gentleman who had lived long in England; he matriculated at Magdalen College, Oxford, and was esteemed as a scholar and as a linguist. I have a copy of the Third Folio edition of Chaucer which once belonged to him and has his signature therein, and there is in the British Museum a copy of the Florio edition of Montaigne which has in it what purports to be the signature of Shakespeare; it was bought about a hundred years ago, for one hundred and forty pounds. With the idea of saving wear and tear on this copy (which turned out to be an eighteenth-century forgery), another copy was bought: this upon examination proved to have been Ben Jonson's copy and has his undoubted signature in it. This is a curious coincidence and was told Emerson when he went to the Museum to see "Shakespeare's Montaigne": these volumes attest the early popularity of the Essayist in England.

Francis Bacon—"the wisest, brightest, meanest of man-kind!" (it has always been my opinion that more damage could be done a man's reputation by a couplet than by a vol-ume of abuse) read Montaigne in French, for in 1597 he published his own *Essays*, some six years before Florio's edition was published. It is a very small octavo volume con-taining ten short papers. Only one copy of the first edition is known and, I think, but one of the second. The title-page of the third edition reads:

ESSAIES
Religious Meditations
Pieces of Persuasion
and Dissuasion
Sceene and Allowed

London, 1598.

In those days the right to print or publish was not easily obtained: "Sceene and Allowed" means that authority saw nothing objectionable in the *Essaies*. Of this edition eleven copies are known; only three of which are in private hands: one of them being in the library of my friend Mr. Carl H. Pforzheimer of New York, where I saw and handled it quite recently. It was this edition of which Harry Widener bought a copy in London a day or two before he sailed in the ill-fated *Titanic*, saying when he did so, "If I should go to the bottom this little book shall go with me." Alas! it did. Edi-tion followed edition, 1598, 1604, 1606, each enlarged; the edition of 1612 is the earliest edition in the "Oak Knoll" Library. It contains "forty little bundles of apothegm"; wise, without a doubt, but as didactic as the devil. Finally the book in its present form appeared in 1632, several years after its author's death. I take it these essays are better known by quotations therefrom than by the papers themselves; they are, in truth, substantial rather than dainty fare. "Some books are to be tasted, others to be swallowed, and some few to be chewed and digested," is a good sample. Few would dispute the truth of Bacon's sayings, but a true essay cannot be made out of sententious statements of fact alone. I have stood, several times, before the statue of Bacon in the parish church of St. Alban's where he is buried: he leaves me cold; one of the outstanding figures in English literature, no one loves him and, notwithstanding his great abilities, few respect him. Emerson, writing a hundred years ago, says: "Bacon has lost half his stature." What if he should some day lose the other half? No worshipper at the shrine of Shakespeare can let slip an opportunity of taking a crack at the mad folk who believe that Francis Bacon wrote the plays attributed to the Bard of Avon; if he did, then Dr. Samuel Johnson wrote *The Pickwick Papers*. And that's flat.

No. The true follower of Montaigne, in English, is not Bacon, but Charles Lamb. He has the humor and benignity without which the essay loses its savor. The perfect essay is as personal as a toothbrush. It is a letter—addressed as letters of recommendation sometimes are—"To whom it may concern"—and it is for the reader to say whether it is intended for him or for another, and as I reflect upon the resemblance of a letter to an essay I am reminded that my friend Mr. E. V. Lucas has somewhere said:

The best letters are those that bring good news, but these are few in comparison to the many that bring you ill. You are expecting a legacy from a man; you hear of his death and at the same time learn that you are overlooked in his will. Or a letter tells you that the job promised you has gone elsewhere. Another that your publisher likes your verses but does not care to print them.

But take the best letters of Walpole, or of Cowper—whose "divine chit-chat" so pleased Charles Lamb that he said he would not call that man friend who should be offended by it —or those of Lamb himself, and we find that we are reading essays charmingly, if at all, disguised.

Macaulay's *Essays*, excellent as they are, are historic or literary studies; their personal qualities, so far as they have any, merely reflect the prejudices of their author. One of his most famous papers is that on Samuel Johnson. It is brilliantly written—a review of a newly edited edition of Boswell's *Life of Johnson*, by John Wilson Croker, of which it purports to be a considered criticism; actually it is full of political hatred. Some time before it appeared Macaulay wrote his sister that Croker's edition of Boswell was soon to appear—that he detested Croker more than cold boiled veal, adding, "See whether I do not dust that varlet's jacket in the next number of the Edinburgh Review." This letter did as much damage to Macaulay's reputation as a critic as any of his many cocksure statements, which when analyzed are seen to be merely eloquence set in motion by prejudice.

Carlyle is another essayist who should be read with caution; the outpourings of an impotent dyspeptic, they flash with genius here and there, certainly, as do those of Macaulay, but they are too frequently tedious and ill tempered, which an essay should never be—when it is, it is a screed, not an essay. I remember well when Carlyle died, back in 1881; it was felt that a great literary light had gone out, and doubtless it had. At the time of his death he enjoyed a reputation not unlike that of Dr. Johnson a century before. Every honor, including lordship, had been offered him; finally they proposed to bury him in the Abbey, but he had preferred the old Kirkyard at Ecclefechan, in Scotland, side by side with his parents. When his *Reminiscences* were published it was seen that his sun was setting, never to rise again. He was steeped in German philosophy, and his *ex cathedra* judgments were usually wrong; lenient with himself, he was bitingly severe on others. His attack on Lamb, who had been dead almost fifty years, was like spitting into the wind. A new generation of critics pointed out that his constant striving for intensity of expression weakened what he designed to be his most emphatic statements. When a man perpetually screams for silence, at the top of his voice, in thirty or more volumes, he at last comes to be regarded chiefly as a nuisance.

In an essay a fact may be stated but there should be nothing controversial:

> For forms of government let fools contest;
> Whate'er is best administered is best.

And was it not my Lord Shaftesbury who said that all wise men were of one religion? And when asked what that was, replied: "Wise men never say." Thus are politics and religion disposed of. But that the best essays have been written in the city, I should have said that the essay could only be written in the country, far away from the noise and distractions of the town. Essays should be reflective; they may contain, and frequently do, traces of humor, but of merriment there should be none. I am thinking of a volume entitled *The Private Papers of Henry Ryecroft*; there was no such person: it was a name assumed by the grim and talented novelist George Gissing, too much of whose sad and sordid life had been spent in a basement of a gloomy tenement in a London slum. A lucky turn of fortune's wheel freed him from want and removed him to Devonshire, where in a sunlit cottage, in a garden, surrounded by his favorite books, he spent his declining years in pleasant meditation. If sorrow's crown of suffering is remembering happier things, as Tennyson tells us it is, looking back upon anxious and hungry hours is well calculated to make one feel as happy in a cottage in Devon as was Horace on his Sabine farm. Not bad advice that of St. Paul to the Thessalonians—whoever they were: to study to be quiet and to mind your own business and to work with your own hands. Voltaire's, curiously enough, is the same: "Let us cultivate our garden."

An essay is, or should be, the work of a poet written in prose. Not all essays are labeled such; nor are all essayists called by that name. The melancholy Jacques in *As You Like It* is an essayist introduced into a play, and his famous soliloquy which begins, "All the world's a stage," is an essay as lovely as it is brief. The first chapter of Thomas Hardy's *Return of the Native* is an essay upon Nature. It is a description of a heath, Egdon Heath; no character moves upon it: it is a great inviolate plain, the trifling irregularities of its surface were not caused by pickaxe, plough, or spade, but have an age which even the sea cannot claim, for who can say of a particular sea that it is old? Distilled by the sun, kneaded by the moon, it is renewed in a year, in a day, in an hour; Egdon Heath remains. I have condensed and compressed a chapter into a paragraph, but I trust I have not distorted what is perhaps the finest description of landscape from the pen of a master. Here is another example. In George Meredith's novel, *The Egoist*, he has a chapter entitled "An Aged and a Great Wine." It is composed very largely of a sparring of two wits: Sir Willoughby Patterne and Dr. Middleton, who in real life was Thomas Love Peacock, Meredith's father-in-law, whose usual style Meredith was imitating. It is a brilliant piece of writing—an essay on the care and drinking of wine. It is too long to quote, but you may take my word for it that it does not fit Dr. Johnson's definition of the word "essay," for in his *Dictionary* he defines an essay as "a loose sally of the mind; an irregular indigested piece; not a regular and orderly composition." I think of the essay in Montaigne's sense: I essay, I do not know, I pause, I weigh, I consider.

It is just fifty years ago that I bought a little volume of essays that I may say, truthfully, gave a slant to my life and which perhaps accounts, in some measure, for my addressing you. The book was published anonymously and its title was *Obiter Dicta*; on its title-page there was an explanation of this unusual title. "An *obiter dictum*," it reads, "in the language of the law, is a gratuitous opinion, an individual impertinence, which, whether it be wise or foolish, right or wrong, bindeth none—not even the lips that utter it." For long no one knew, with the possible exception of the publishers, the author of it: when I discovered that it was written by a man named Augustine Birrell, I was little wiser than before—the name meant nothing to me, but the book meant much; it opened to me a new art, the art of the essay. The volume contained seven little papers and a preface to the American edition which read as follows:

This seems a very little book to introduce to so large a continent. No such enterprise would ever have suggested itself to the home-keeping mind of the Author, who, none the less, when this edition was proposed to him by Messrs. Scribner on terms honorable to them and grateful to him, found the notion of being read in America most fragrant and delightful.

I found the little volume "fragrant and delightful," and I find it so today. The first English edition of this book, which is rare, was published privately, and the essays are prefaced by a number of little poems of doubtful merit. It was followed from time to time by a number of other small volumes, all in the same vein. Wise and witty criticisms, new appraisements of old books and of old authors. Meantime Birrell was getting up in the world. He "took silk," became a Bencher of the Inner Temple and Professor of Law at University College, London. Finally he became popular as an after-dinner speaker, and, unluckily, a politician; he was Chief Secretary of Ireland when the Great War broke out. All went well for a time, then came the treason of Sir Roger Casement, with its accompanying fighting in Dublin. Birrell should have been "Birrelling" with his books in London, not trying to stop Sinn Fein riots in Ireland, a job for which he was totally unfitted. He failed utterly; manfully he made his explanations in the House of Commons. He spoke, he said, "amid the ruin of his hopes and aspirations." That was the end of his public career; he returned to his books—to Dr. Johnson, and Hannah More, and Carlyle, Browning, and Newman, and many more. Of all men, and women too, he wrote as though he had with them a personal acquaintance; his style charmed thousands.

I little thought that the time would come when Birrell and I would become, if not intimate friends, at least friendly enough to exchange letters, to bandy words, one with another face to face, and to raise a glass of wine to one another across a dinner table in the attic room of the Johnson House in Gough Square, of which house we both were made trustees by our common friend, Cecil Harmsworth. The penultimate time we met I gave him a little luncheon at my club in London, and we, with one or two others, sat until late in the afternoon talking of men, women, and books, after the manner of our kind. I shall not soon forget that delightful afternoon. Another of my guests was Holbrook Jackson, the author of *The Anatomy of Bibliomania*. I know no book like it. It is an assemblage of brief essays, all that has been written through the ages about the writing, the collecting, and the reading of books, brought together in the quaint style of "Old Burton," he of the *Melancholy* fame. Gosh! and likewise Glory! What a book. The making of it was the relaxation of a busy editor for twenty years or so. Until I came to know Jackson well I thought of him, not as one man but as a "synod" of men. Finally we had to call it a day and I put Birrell into a taxi and took him to his home in Chelsea, for he was by now an old man and did not enjoy going about the crowded streets of London in the twilight, alone. The last time we met was in the aforementioned attic room at a meeting of the Johnson Club, when after the usual supper some stupid man began to read a paper on the Chief Justices of Dr. Johnson's time—a paper with slides. You know how deadly dull such a paper can be when it is

badly delivered, when the slides come in, as they occasionally did on this occasion, upside down, or when accompa-
nied by "We have here a portrait of Lord Mansfield,"
whereupon the slide showed not Lord Mansfield but his
residence, Kenwood, in the north of London. Birrell had become by now a gritty old party, he never suffered fools
gladly; on this occasion he declined to suffer interminably,
and after an hour, saying in a stage whisper, "I can stand
this no longer," he proceeded to stalk out of the room to the
stairs where, releasing his cane he let it slide down with a
thump and a bump on every step, most people thinking it
was the owner and not the stick which was thus descending;
anyhow it served to bring the meeting to an end.

You will pardon this long aside—I had intended to tell
you that one of the papers in *Obiter Dicta* is entitled "Truth
Hunting": it is, in fact, an appreciation of Charles Lamb—
rather at the expense of the unlovely, if greatly gifted Samuel Taylor Coleridge. I rather think that before reading
this paper Charles Lamb was known to me as the author of
The Essays of Elia, but who or what Elia was, I am afraid I
did not know, and of Coleridge I knew less. I have read this
essay so often that it has remained almost entire in the col-
ander I call my memory. May I indulge myself in a long
quotation?

I believe I run no great risk in asserting that, of all English
authors, Charles Lamb is the one loved most warmly and emo-
tionally by his admirers, amongst whom I reckon only those who
are as familiar with the four volumes of his "Life and Letters" as
with "Elia."

Speaking of his sister Mary, who, as everyone knows, throughout "Elia" is called his Cousin Bridget, he says:

"It has been the lot of my cousin, oftener, perhaps, than I could have wished, to have had for her associates and mine free-thinkers, leaders and disciples of novel philosophies and systems, but she neither wrangles with nor accepts their opinions."

Nor did her brother. He lived his life cracking his little jokes and reading his great folios, neither wrangling with nor accepting the opinions of the friends he loved to see around him. To a contemporary stranger it might well have appeared as if his life were a frivolous and useless one as compared with those of these philosophers and thinkers. *They* discussed their great schemes and affected to probe deep mysteries, and were constantly asking, "What is Truth?" *He* sipped his glass, shuffled his cards, and was content with the humbler inquiry, "What are trumps?" But to us, looking back upon that little group, and knowing what we now do about each member of it, no such mistake is possible. To us it is plain beyond all question that, judged by whatever standard of excellence it is possible for any reasonable human being to take, Lamb still stands head and shoulders a better man than any of them. No need to stop to compare him with Godwin, or Hazlitt, or Lloyd; let us boldly put him in the scales with one whose fame is in all the churches—with Samuel Taylor Coleridge, "logician, metaphysician, bard."

.   .   .   .   .   .

In early manhood Coleridge planned a Pantisocracy where all the virtues were to thrive. Lamb did something far more difficult: he played cribbage every night with his imbecile father, whose constant stream of querulous talk and fault-finding might well have goaded a far stronger man into practising and justifying neglect.

.   .   .   .   .   .

Coleridge married. Lamb, at the bidding of duty, remained single, wedding himself to the sad fortunes of his father and sister. Shall we pity him? No; he had his reward—the surpassing reward that is only within the power of literature to bestow. It was Lamb, and not Coleridge, who wrote "Dream-Children: a Reverie":

"Then I told how for seven long years, in hope sometimes, sometimes in despair, yet persisting ever, I courted the fair Alice W——n; and as much as children could understand, I explained to them what coyness and difficulty and denial meant in maidens —when, suddenly turning to Alice, the soul of the first Alice looked out at her eyes with such a reality of representment that I became in doubt which of them stood before me, or whose that bright hair was; and while I stood gazing, both the children gradually grew fainter to my view, receding and still receding, till nothing at last but two mournful features were seen in the uttermost distance, which, without speech, strangely impressed upon me the effects of speech. 'We are not of Alice nor of thee, nor are we children at all. The children of Alice call Bartrum father. We are nothing, less than nothing, and dreams. We are only what might have been.' "

Godwin! Hazlitt! Coleridge! Where now are their "novel philosophies and systems"? Bottled moonshine, which does *not* improve by keeping.

That essay made me an Elian, and when, forty years later, a lucky stroke of business enabled me to buy one of my most valued literary possessions, the original manuscript of "Dream Children," I felt very proud indeed. It had once belonged to Harry B. Smith, and in his delightful book, *First Nights and First Editions*, he says: "Only once have I paid more than a thousand dollars for a book or an autograph: that was when I gave a London dealer two hundred and twenty-five pounds for Lamb's 'Dream Children.' I do not know who owns it now, but he would probably consider ten thousand dollars a low price for it." He would indeed, Mr. Smith, very low.

I venture to think that no one since Lamb has written a better essay than "Truth Hunting." I am not letter perfect in Lamb—I am not letter perfect in anything—but I submit that the essays of Charles Lamb, under whatever title they are published, are, at their best, far and away the finest essays we have in English. Christopher North is merely a name; of De Quincey nothing is remembered except his *Opium Eater*, which is not properly an essay. "We are all fine fellows but we can't write like Hazlitt," exclaims, in a burst of enthusiasm, Robert Louis Stevenson. Well, Hazlitt is remembered by half a dozen excellent essays: "On Going a Journey" is one, "The Fight" is another, "My First Acquaintance with the Poets" is a third; you may select the other three. As I was writing these lines on the day before Christmas last, a servant entered my library and handed me a number of letters and a small parcel; I opened the parcel first, I prefer presents to letters; what do you think it was? —a slender book, printed in, of all places in the world, Woodstock, Vermont, entitled *The Fight, An Essay by William Hazlitt*, with a colored frontispiece; and on the flyleaf was written, "A Christmas Greeting from Maud and Otis Skinner." And when my hand became tired holding the pen I renewed my acquaintance with the story of the essayist going down into the country to see the famous prize fight between Tom Hickman, the Gas Man, so called, and Bill Neate. Not many prize fights have been described by such an essayist as Hazlitt. It was to carry on this tradition that a few years ago John Drinkwater came from London to New York to report and describe a fight between Carpen-

tier, a Frenchman, and another heavy-weight, Dempsey, I
think. But I know little about prize fighters.

"There is more reason for saying grace before a good
book than before a good dinner," says Charles Lamb. The
same may be said of an essay. The essay should be more or
less autobiographical, not stiff with learning, but wise, witty,
and tender, designed, as Caxton said reading should be,
"for to make the time to pass pleasantly" and so carefully
wrought that the skill that entered into its making is entirely concealed. How hard this is to do is evidenced by the
few essays that survive the generation in which they are
written. Or to state the fact another way, to write a good
essay is either easy or impossible. Lamb and Wordsworth
were talking about Shakespeare one evening, when the poet
said "he could write like Shakespeare if he had a mind to."
"That's all you need, William," said Lamb, "the mind."
One final word as to "Dream Children." There was,
some years ago, at the Wesleyan University in Middle-
town, Connecticut, a professor of English and a fine essayist, Dr. C. T. Winchester. His volume, *An Old Castle*, is
one of the best volumes of literary essays I know; the old
castle is Ludlow, on the Welsh border, where Milton's famous mask *Comus* was produced for the first time by the children of the Earl of Bridgewater, whose home the castle was.
And in another volume, entitled *A Group of English Essayists*, Winchester, speaking of Lamb, says:

Only once or twice—perhaps only once, in that most intimate
of all his essays, the *Dream Children*—does Lamb drop all affec-
tations and tell us the things that lay nearest his heart in
language too utterly sincere even for the disguise of his "self-

pleasing quaintness." In that perfect essay humor is quite lost in pathos; and the English in which the simple story is told, for purity of idiom, chaste simplicity, and artless grace of movement, is quite unsurpassed. No one else in Lamb's day wrote such English, and to find anything so perfect you will have to go back to the best passages of the English Bible. Here Lamb has set up a glass where we may see the inmost part of him.

Indeed it may be said with confidence that no paragraph in any English essay is as beautiful as the last half dozen lines of "Dream Children." They have been set to music. Their contemplation suggested to the late Sir Edward Elgar two brief pieces of orchestral music, which have, I am told—for I do not know of my own knowledge—a delicacy and wistful beauty for which that great composer was famous. What would Charles Lamb have said to this? He, who wrote "I have no ear," and then went on to explain that he was not speaking architecturally, he meant *for music*; that he was quite incapable of carrying a tune, that all his life he had been practising at odd moments and in solitary corners "God Save the King," yet had not arrived, at the time of writing, within many quavers of it.

I am loath to leave the subject: Lamb in his "Detached Thoughts on Books and Reading" says: "Much depends upon *when* and *where* you read a book. . . . Milton almost requires a solemn service of music before you enter upon him." The essayist makes no such demand, you may dip into him how and when you will, in the five or six impatient minutes before dinner time which would otherwise be wasted, or, worse—used for grumbling.

I shall not pretend that this paper was prepared without some care, and as I read over my rough notes it suddenly occurred to me to re-read a volume of essays by Alexander Smith, an almost forgotten Scotchman, who is remembered, if he is remembered, by one small volume of essays called *Dreamthorp*, published before I was born. I have a first edition of this book, and taking it from its place on my shelves I opened it and to my amazement read in a paper entitled "On the Writing of Essays" much that I have said about Montaigne; this is not surprising, for everything that can be said about Montaigne has been said—as about Shakespeare: the only thing that remains is to say it in a new way. But I also came upon this: "Jacques in 'As You Like It' has the making of a charming essayist" and "the essayist is a kind of poet in prose." I was not consciously pilfering from Alexander Smith when I wrote, a few days before, identically the same thing. I don't think I have dipped into *Dreamthorp* for several years; I read *As You Like It* only a few weeks ago, and I was struck at the time that the romantic Jacques, who is usually lying under a greenwood tree when he delivers his famous soliloquy, would have been a fine essayist if he had not been a finer thing—a fine poet. Reading further on, I came upon this: "It is not the essayist's duty to inform . . . incidentally he may do something in that way just as the poet may, but it is not his duty." I was just going to labor this point, and I shall not be turned aside from the fact that a better man than I has done it before me.

I have an old volume published in London in 1793, entitled *Essays, Humorous, Moral and Literary, chiefly in the manner of The Spectator* by Benjamin Franklin: these are not essays, as I understand the word, they are little sermons rather, all the better for being brief: they were intended to teach, to improve our conduct, a very excellent thing in itself, but nothing could be further from the purpose of an essay. And if I am right as to Dr. Franklin's papers "in the manner of The Spectator," Dr. Johnson's papers in the manner of himself will hardly pass muster as essays. His ponderous tomes, *The Rambler* and *The Idler*, which look so well in their original calf upon our shelves, are seldom removed except to be dusted and replaced. No, we prefer *The Spectator* himself, and we prefer *The Tatler* to *The Spectator*. Why? Because its object was "to enlighten morality with wit and to temper wit with morality," and the result was that fine old gentleman Sir Roger de Coverley and his friend Will Honeycomb. Ah, Dick Steele! you were an essayist we would all stem from an' we could. Do you remember the letter he wrote to his wife Prue? his second wife—he met her at the funeral of his first. "Dear Prue," it reads, "I am too drunk to go home but not too drunk to send you my love." I quote from memory. Dicky, later Sir Richard Steele, was always in debt and difficulty, and perhaps as the world rolls on and fills up with things we must or should remember, he may be recalled, chiefly, by the magnificent compliment he once paid to a lady of whom he said that "to love her is a liberal education." I have always maintained that there is immortality in a couplet or a line.

The essay is a slender thread upon which to hang a lasting reputation; that Alexander Smith's *Dreamthorp* is still read after seventy years speaks well for its longer survival. "On the Importance of a Man to Himself" is the suggestive title of one of his papers. "A man strikes it [the world] with all his might . . . forty thousand pounds, a peerage and Westminster Abbey," is his demand. He gets them all; is he happy? not necessarily, or even probably. When the captains and the kings of this generation depart, the essayist departs with them and is forgotten. In Washington and in London and in Paris, where reputations are made more quickly than elsewhere, they are most quickly forgotten; to be happy and to be remembered one should live behind the times and so propel himself into the future. The subject was once suggested to me by Owen Wister as suggesting an essay, but I am not equal to it: it would have suited Alexander Smith perfectly. Certainly we live too much in the present, getting and spending, we lay waste our powers—a common fault—it is especially so with us. Had we been wiser we should have had taxes small or none; as it is, we are told that we should be content because England's are heavier than ours. Compare England's size and age with ours and let us blush at our stupidity.

I am thinking of Oliver Goldsmith, of whom Dr. Johnson said, "Is there a man now living who can pen an essay with such ease and elegance as Dr. Goldsmith?" His essays would be better remembered than they are but for the beauty of his verse. I find an essay concealed in almost every line of his *Deserted Village*; take the picture of the tavern where the

> . . . village statesmen talked with looks profound
> And news much older than their ale went round.

I shall never forget one day when in a little town of Tewkesbury, in England, I took refuge from the cold in its great abbey, which is almost a cathedral; it seemed to be heated only by some candles which stood round the coffin of a man whose funeral service was going on; for a time I participated. An hour later I entered the Black Bear public house

for a long drink of something strong and hot, for I was per-
ishing. Seated in the taproom round a tiny fire was a group
of old men who stopped talking about the funeral when I
entered, but made room for me to sit down. Presently one
of the men took up the conversation where, seemingly, it
has been broken off when I came in, and remarked:

"They do say as 'ow 'e's left her a thousan' poun'."

"A thousan' poun'! she won't stay a widdy long; not
with a thousan' poun'," remarked another.

"I'd marry 'er for less," said a very old man, taking a
pipe out of an almost toothless mouth.

"With what?" said a man, determined to be facetious.

"With a ring, o' course."

Evidently the village wit.

> Full well they laughed with counterfeited glee,
> At all his jokes, for many a joke had he.

But I am wandering from my text, as is my habit.

The generation that I am addressing which enjoys the
automobile and the radio can hardly understand the respect
the generation to which I seem to belong had for the name
of Ralph Waldo Emerson—I say "seem to belong," for it
may be that I straddle two generations, belonging to neither. We, manufacturers of electrical machinery, rather
questioned his prophetic judgment when he inquired, "Of
what value is the electric spark? it is the toy of the labora-
tory": this only a few years before the "electric spark" became busy changing every detail of life throughout the entire world; nevertheless Emerson's was a name to conjure
with. Now, if we think of him at all, we think of him as belonging to what Mr. Roosevelt called the horse and buggy

age. If we judge it by any other standard than that of the inventor, it was superior to our own. In the matter of love-making, for example, authorities are generally agreed that courting could be well carried on in a buggy, motivated by a horse that could be trusted to mind his own business and say nothing. With a horse, progress, if slow, was sure; whereas, to make love, safely, in a motor car, the machine has to be parked on the roadside: you may have observed the phenomenon. It is to be regretted that we cannot gear our machines one speed forward and two reverse. *Festina lente*, make haste slowly, is an excellent motto.

I wonder, sometimes, whether we Americans sufficiently realize the popularity of our own essayist, Washington Irving, for it is as an essayist that he is chiefly remembered. He was our first man of letters, accepted and known abroad about the time that Sydney Smith was sneering, "Who reads an American book?" The answer is, "We do," and not we only, but all who read the relatively easy European languages, as well as those who express themselves in Czech, Greek, Polish, Russian, Yiddish, and Welsh, for into all these languages *The Sketch Book* has been translated. The first edition of this *Sketch Book*—for its bibliographical intricacies William R. Langfeld of this city is the authority—is excessively rare, as a book published in seven paper-cover pamphlets a hundred and fifteen years ago must inevitably be. How little could its author have foreseen that this item would become, and deservedly, one of the most sought of collectors' items, not alone because of its rarity, as Poe's *Tamerlane* is, but because of its enduring charm. *Bracebridge Hall*, which followed it, is also a lovely cluster of essays, and if Squire Bracebridge is a lineal descendant of Sir

Roger de Coverley, let it be remembered that Irving discovered Christmas a generation before Charles Dickens wrote the *Carol*. But the essay by which Irving will be remembered longest is "Rip Van Winkle"; I might be within bounds in saying that of all the essays in the language it is one of the best known. What other essay has been turned into a play which held the stage for more than a generation, and still enshrines the name of a fine old actor? There are compensations for age, and the recollection of Joe Jefferson as Rip Van Winkle is one of them. But I confess that I would cheerfully forego this recollection could I own the manuscript of *The Sketch Book*, including "Rip," as my friend and neighbor Boies Penrose does.

Edgar Allan Poe, perhaps our outstanding literary figure, is at the same time the most baffling. A poet, full of sound, if not of fury, signifying almost nothing; a writer of "tales" equaled by few and surpassed by none, it is as an essayist, if anything, that he is, as James Russell Lowell said, "three-fifths of him genius and two-fifths sheer fudge." And to quote Lowell again, if he sometimes mistakes a bottle of prussic acid for an inkwell he nevertheless wrote critical essays quite as excellent as any of the same sort then being produced in England. I am thinking of those vitriolic essays which came from Edinburgh about a century ago, violently wrong as criticism and useless as anything else.

One turns with a sense of relief to Donald G. Mitchell—Ik. Marvel, as he called himself—whose *Reveries of a Bachelor* remains a pleasant, if slightly sentimental picture of a happily married man (he had eleven children and God knows how many grandchildren) crooning over the ashes of a wood fire; was it oak or hickory he affected? I forget—

enjoying and making others enjoy the view out of his window, his books, his tobacco, and his fancied loneliness. With him we enjoy "Dream Life" and a "Wet Day at Edgewood," his farm, once on the outskirts of New Haven, now no doubt a part of that bustling and very foreign city in which, except in the purlieus of Yale, one hardly hears English spoken. How mongrel this nation has become! In Salem, Massachusetts, a year or two ago, I was looking for the Old Manse, celebrated by Hawthorne for its mosses (there's another essayist and a good one). Will you believe me? the first three or four people to whom I applied for directions did not speak English. But they vote, no doubt early and often, as their boss tells them to.

In the preparation of this address I took down my Emerson and read or attempted to read several volumes, once favorites of mine. The volume *Representative Men* I found to be tedious, if not tiresome. "The American Scholar," an address delivered a hundred years ago before the Phi Beta Kappa Society—a society of which I am an honorary member—I had years ago enthusiastically marked; today I wonder why. A hundred years ago we were debating questions that we are debating still. "Temperance" for example—today we call it "Prohibition." Then we were debating "The Power of the Executive" and "The Power of the Banks" and the "Tariff"—and are we not debating them still?

> Myself when young did eagerly frequent
> Doctor and Saint and heard great argument
> About it and about: but evermore
> Came out by the same door where in I went.

I conclude that Emerson, like his friend Thomas Carlyle, did not write essays so much as "Tracts for the Times."

Thirty years ago I thought Oscar Wilde's "The Soul of Man Under Socialism" a brilliant essay; today I find it nothing but a highly wrought bundle of paradoxes. When an essay is timely it is lost, but Charles Lamb's essay on "Old China," which wanders from a pagoda on a plate to a bookseller's in Islington, to the theatre in Drury Lane and back again, is not likely to grow outmoded.

There is another essayist of the old school of whom I must say a word, Richard Le Gallienne. He is living today and wrote a review of a book by a friend of mine which was published in the *New York Times*, only a few weeks ago. The book reviewed was *The Voice of England*, by Professor Osgood of Princeton University. It is a history of English Literature from the earliest to the present time and is in fact a volume of several thousand little essays, each a flower, bound together by a string, a thread, a cord, as old Montaigne calls it, of the Professor's own devising. I am not unfamiliar with histories of literature, which is the noblest thing man has produced: when you wish to hear a symphony listen to *The Voice of England*. But to Le Gallienne. A volume lies before me which was once Swinburne's. It is called *Travels in England*. Now, books of travel in general do not interest me any more than do medical, or law books, except Blackstone. The peculiarity of Le Gallienne's travels is that the author seldom arrives at his destination. It is no more a book of travels in the accepted sense than is Lamb's "Oxford in Vacation" an excerpt from Baedeker; indeed one of his essays is entitled "Avoiding Stonehenge." But he meanders through a lovely countryside, putting up at old inns, talking to quaint characters, supping on bread and cheese with a mug of ale, smoking a pipe, reading a book and go-

ing to bed. Open the book where you will, you will find little bits which seem to have been written for you alone. It is
the letter over again. Take the chapter on Winchester Cathedral. Who cares that William Rufus, shot a-hunting in
the New Forest, is buried in a tomb of basalt under the
great tower; what we want to see is the spot where King
Canute, that silly Dane, is buried. He who, flattered by his
courtiers, rebuked them by issuing vain commands against
a rising tide, according to the legend. Is that William
Rufus's tomb? Good. R.I.P. Rip, let him rest! but forget
not the chapel in which the world's greatest Angler, properly
an essayist, reposes; or the black slab which covers all that
could die of the author of *Pride and Prejudice*. One travels
far without the inconvenience of locomotion when such
names occur to one.

And there is Winterslow Hutt, where Hazlitt, the grandfather of the cantankerous Hazlitt, lived for a time and did
some of his finest work. The place is nothing, or next to it,
but as Le Gallienne says, "It is something to see a place
where something was really written, a place where the fire
once came down, is a good deal—or nothing at all, as one
happens to be constituted." I am so constituted and have
gone more than once to see the place where the fire came
down on the Brontës, in the rectory at Haworth; and on
Thomas Hardy, on Egdon Heath; and on Anthony Trollope at Salisbury, for there he conceived the idea of *The
Warden*, although actually the Hospital of St. Cross, a mile
or two out of Winchester, is the locale of that lovely idyll.
But the danger of looking for such fireplaces is very real;
too often they lead to disappointment. This, however, is the
subject for an essay: some day I hope to tamper with it.

In a different vein are the essays of the late George Moore. Here again the novelist outshines the essayist, but one essay in particular gives me great joy. It is called "Royalty in Art" in a volume entitled *Modern Painting*. It is an attack upon the taste of Queen Victoria and her family.

The private taste of Royalty creates the public taste of the nation, and the public result of the interest that the Queen was pleased to take in Sir Edgar Boehm, a German,—she made him an English knight,—is the disfigurement of London by several of the worst statues it is possible to conceive. The ancient site of Temple Bar has been disfigured by Boehm with statues of the Queen and the Prince of Wales, so stupidly conceived and so stupidly modelled that they look like figures out of Noah's ark. The finest site in London, Hyde Park Corner, has been disfigured by Boehm with a statue of the Duke of Wellington so bad, so paltry, so characteristically the work of a German mechanic, that it is impossible to drive down the beautiful road without experiencing a sensation of discomfort and annoyance. A city so naturally beautiful as London can do without statues; the question is not so much how to get good statues, but how to protect London against bad statues. If for the next twenty-five years we might celebrate the memory of each great man by the destruction of a statue, we might undo a great part of the mischief for which Royalty is mainly responsible.

It would ill become me as a Philadelphian to leave the subject of the essay without special reference to our one outstanding literary figure: I refer, of course, to Agnes Repplier. We have watched her style expand and ripen until she has certainly no superior and few equals as an essayist. Being a woman she has not been able to enjoy the privileges of a man; if she has taken the wind of the world she has not

knocked about in it, hence her papers lack the autobiographical quality which I contend the essay should have.
Nor can she say with Charles Lamb: "I cannot sit and think,
books think for me," for the lady has trained herself to do
her own thinking and her own method of expression. She
can fight battles for what she believes to be the right—and
I seldom disagree with her—and her weapons are wit, irony,
and sarcasm; in debate God help the man who disagrees
with her. As I look at the row of little volumes which rep-
resent her life's work, a conversation I once had in London
occurs to me. It was in a bookshop that a man, whom I
knew to be a scholar, hearing that I came from Philadelphia,
asked me "Did I know Agnes Repplier?" I replied, not
boastingly I hope, that "I did, very well." "Then," said my
interlocutor, "you know the best and clearest writer of the
English essay we have today." His choice of her books was
not mine; you will wish to know mine. *To Think of Tea* is
delightful. So is *A Happy Half Century*—that is to say,
from the last twenty-five years of the eighteenth century to
the end of the first twenty-five years of the nineteenth.
Goldsmith died at the beginning of it, Cowper in the middle, Lamb at the end. Democracy had not yet been taken
seriously, and an excellent literary reputation could be had,
if not for the asking, certainly for the taking. Those golden
days are gone; we live in a distracting and destructed world.
But, as the English Tommy sang during the late unpleas-
antness: "It's a terrible, terrible, terrible war, still it is better than no war at all." And so I say of the world.

It is customary for a lecturer to end upon a note of opti-
mism. In my best "fireside manner" then, and in my nearest approach to a Harvard voice—"My friends, let me give

you a word of comfort. These papers, the preparation of which has been a pleasant task, are at an end: time and the hour has run through the roughest day."

May I tell you one more story?—a brief one. Some fifty-six or seven years agone, I was a boy in a famous book-store in Philadelphia. One very hot summer day a clergyman entered. He wore a high choker collar and a long black coat and a hat about three inches high, with a broad brim. One would suspect a man of treason or of arson who would on such a day out-rig himself in such a silly costume—but let that pass. One of the salesmen in the store, who knew him well, went up to him while he was mopping his face with his handkerchief and said, "Well, Doctor, how would you like to preach a sermon on a day like this?" The Doctor paused for a moment and then in an august manner—well suited to the day—replied: "I should always prefer to preach a sermon rather than listen to one." "My friends," I do not always find myself in entire agreement with clergymen, but I should always prefer to deliver a lecture rather than listen to one.